Never Sleep Alone

Never Sleep Alone

Dr. Alex Schiller

G
Gallery Books
New York   London   Toronto   Sydney   New Delhi

G

Gallery Books

A Division of Simon & Schuster, Inc.

1230 Avenue of the Americas
New York, NY 10020

First Gallery Books trade paperback edition February 2015

Interior design by Davina Mock-Maniscalco
The interior photos in the STAR chapter are by Jesse Ditmar.
NSA Truth and NSA Challenge graphics by Mark Bunker.

Manufactured in the United States of America

10   9   8   7   6   5   4   3   2   1

Library of Congress Cataloging-in-Publication Data

Hart, Roslyn.
  Never sleep alone / Dr. Alex Schiller.
    pages cm
  1. Sex—Humor. 2. Man-woman relationships—Humor. 3. Single people—
Humor. 4. Dating (Social custom)—Humor. I. Title.
  PN6231.S54.H37 2015
  818'.602—dc23
                                                    2014008659

ISBN 978-1-4767-4132-1
ISBN 978-1-4767-4133-8 (ebook)

This book is dedicated to the beautiful person
who gave me the most intense orgasm of my life.
You know who you are.

CONTENTS

Contents

WELCOME TO NSA

YOU HAVE FOUND NSA at the perfect moment in your life and you must begin immediately.

———

Tomorrow your genitals could turn to dust.

Don't waste the best years of your life being fearful and mediocre. It is time to overcome your inhibitions, transform your existence, and become the Exceptional Individual you were meant to be.

I want to help you.

I want to help you feel better than you have ever felt in your entire life. I want to help you become your most beautiful and powerful self, so that you will never feel lonely or hungry or horny again.

I am often asked, "Dr. Alex, how do I find The One? How do I find that perfect person who makes me feel complete?"

My answer to that question is always the same:

To find The One, you must *become* The One.

WHEN YOU ARE The One, you never want for anything, because you are always being given everything. When you are The One, you never chase after sex, romance, or love— because everyone is always chasing after YOU.

When you are The One, you Never Sleep Alone.

Unless you want to.

You don't have to sleep with everyone.

But everyone is going to want to sleep with you.

And when everyone wants to sleep with you, you have the power to get whatever you want.

NSA is a philosophy consisting of 9 NSA Principles that, when fully actualized, are guaranteed to transform you into The One that everyone wants.

Do exactly as I tell you, without hesitation or expectations, and you shall not fail.

Let us begin.

PREPARE YOURSELF

YOU ARE ABOUT TO go on an amazing journey.

You are going to have new experiences, you are going to visit exotic places, you are going to meet beautiful people, and these people are going to want to sleep with you.

If this is hard for you to believe, then you are just like everybody else. And because you are just like everybody else, almost nobody wants to sleep with you.

NSA TRUTH

People only want to sleep with people who are better than they are.

The good news is:

> 98 percent of the population is mediocre.
>
> Do you know what that means?

> **me·di·o·cre** - *adj* mē-dē-'ō-kər\
> of only ordinary or moderate quality; neither
> good nor bad; barely adequate

> That's you.
>
> Yes, *you*.
>
> You are barely adequate.
>
> You inspire no strong emotions or passionate reactions

from the people around you.

But fear not. Most people are mediocre. And most of those mediocre people have *no idea* they are mediocre. Did you know you were mediocre before I told you?

You're welcome.

By actively taking steps to transform yourself, while the rest of the Mediocre Majority stay exactly as they are, you immediately become better than most people, which will make most people want to sleep with you.

From this point forward, we are going to focus on raising you above the Mediocre Majority and transforming you into an *Exceptional Individual.* Do you know what "exceptional" means?

> **ex·cep·tion·al** - *adj* ik-'sep-shə-nəl\
> well above average; unusual, extraordinary,
> different from others

This book contains several NSA Challenges, which you must complete before proceeding to the next NSA Principle. If you truly complete every NSA Challenge while fully and consistently actualizing the 9 NSA Principles, you *will* become an Exceptional Individual whom everyone wants to sleep with.

You will become The One.

If you don't, you won't.

I personally complete each NSA Challenge several times a year and update NeverSleepAlone.com regularly with my latest results. As a sociosexual scientist, I am curious to see what effect different variables have on the NSA Challenges. Sometimes I wear my hair differently, sometimes I pretend to be deaf, and sometimes I dress like a man and seduce an older woman, or a pair of young gay brothers.

Feel free to experiment.

You can read the results of my NSA Challenges at NeverSleepAlone.com—I can't wait to read yours.

If you do not complete the challenges, you will not fully actualize the 9 NSA Principles, and you will not complete your transformation.

If you find the NSA Program too difficult, you can always move to a third-world country and bring clean water to poor people who will sleep with you. But, for right now, while you're living in this beautiful developed country, I want you to do your best to be all that you can be.

NSA Principle 1

NSA = NSA

Never Sleep Alone = No Strings Attached

IF YOU WANT TO Never Sleep Alone (NSA), you must actualize the principle of No Strings Attached (NSA). Which means:

You must be OPEN to every new experience.

and

You must have NO EXPECTATIONS for any experience.

It's that simple.

If you can truly master this one lesson, you will become better than most people, which will make most people want to sleep with you.

Most people are not open to new experiences. Most people would never go on a vacation to Brazil by themselves. Most people are not brave enough to meet their former high school teacher for a late-night drink. Most people are cowards who say no when the busboy invites them to a disco party. Most people say no when their mother's friend offers them a blow job.

You say, "That's not me! I say yes all the time!"

Liar.

You say no more than you say yes. And because you have such a limited number of new experiences, you approach each new experience with multiple unrealistic expectations.

On the rare occasion when you *are* open to a new experience, like most people, *you are expecting a certain outcome.* You're expecting the person you asked to dinner to "make the reach." You're expecting the person you went down on last night to call you again. You're expecting to find the love of your life.

And when your ridiculous expectations are not met, you believe you have failed. This feeling of failure keeps you from actively seeking more new experiences, and this continued lack of new experiences just leads to more unrealistic expectations.

It is a vicious cycle from which you must break free.

NSA TRUTH

A shortage of experiences
will lead to a surplus of expectations.

Expectations are poison. They make you feel anxious, they make you look unattractive, and they make it nearly impossible for you to give and receive MBOs.

Mind-
Blowing
Orgasm

Do you want to have Mind-Blowing Orgasms?

Then you must learn to have No Expectations.

After my live seminar, there is always someone who comes up to me and asks, "How am I supposed to have No Expectations? It's impossible!"

I say to this person, "Take off your shirt."

They comply.

I then ask, "What are you expecting to happen now?"

They say, nervously, "I really don't know."

I then put a hundred-dollar bill in their hand and ask again, "What are you expecting to happen now?"

Now happy, they again say, "I really don't know."

I then say, "Take off your pants."

They hesitate.

I then take a wad of hundred-dollar bills out of my pocket and start counting the money.

They immediately take off their pants.

A crowd begins to form around them.

I then ask again, "What are you expecting to happen now?"

They reply, quite excited, "I really don't know."

I then say, "You have No Expectations?"

This person, now nearly naked and quite happy, answers, "I have No Expectations!"

I then snatch the hundred-dollar bill from their hand,

throw a glass of water in their face, turn on my heel, and walk away, with all of the money and all of their clothes. My bodyguard takes them roughly by the arm and escorts them outside as everyone in the room watches.

Sometimes the person protests, sometimes the person starts crying, sometimes the person shouts, "You stupid, crazy bitch!"

My bodyguard takes them to a waiting limousine, makes them get into the backseat alone, and slams the door. On the seat are their clothes and one thousand dollars in cash.

After thirty seconds, I get into the backseat with them and ask, "What are you expecting to happen now?"

They say, truthfully this time, "I have No Expectations."

I then give them a Mind-Blowing Orgasm.

I do this to prove the following NSA Truth:

NSA TRUTH

*The only way to stop having expectations
is to start having more new experiences.*

The more new experiences you have, the more you realize that it is impossible to predict outcomes. The more new things you do, and the more new people you sleep with, the more you begin to realize that it is pointless to have expectations, because *you can't control nature and you can't control other people.*

You can't even control yourself right now.

If you could, you would make yourself have No Expectations.

See how that works?

Starting today, you are going to *try everything and expect nothing.* You are going to visit new places, meet new people, and experiment with music, fashion, food, and sexual preferences. Every month, you are going to leave your hometown and go somewhere you have *never* been. Every day, you are going to strive to do at least three things you have *never* done before. All the things you used to think about doing or talk about doing—you are going to start doing those things.

Right now.

These new experiences can be as simple as going to a new grocery store, taking a different route to work, or going on a blind date. Or they can be as complex as taking an Asian cooking course, quitting your job, or participating in an interracial threesome at a French rodeo.

Did you know there are rodeos in France?

There are.

I'm at one right now.

And I'm talking to a tall black man and a petite Russian woman.

Put the book down and go have at least one new experience. I don't want to feel your fingers again until you do.

Go.

The Look of Expectation vs. The Aura of Experience

Have you ever noticed that it is always the people you do *not* want to sleep with who really *do* want to sleep with you? That is because when you are with those people, you want nothing from them. You have No Expectations for the person or the situation, and this makes you devastatingly attractive.

NSA TRUTH

Want nothing from no one and everyone will want to give you everything.

When you expect something from a person or situation, you have a certain look on your face. I call this *The Look of Expectation.* You look like a crippled and forlorn hound, desperately hunting for a bone. Or a scabbed leper with an asymmetrical face and creepy eyes, knotted hand held out, begging for a coin, or a crust of bread, or a kind word, or a bed for the night—*anything* to make your pathetic life better . . .

YOU.

LOOK.

NEEDY.

Where have you seen that look before?

You've seen it on that person who really wants you, who really *needs* you, even though you have no desire or need for them.

It's gross.

NSA TRUTH

Neediness is the most unattractive
quality in a human being.

But when you allow yourself to experience something with *No Expectations*, you give off a special glow. I call this *The Aura of Experience*.

When you have *The Aura of Experience*, you radiate the inner peace of an Exceptional Individual. You appear otherworldly, beyond human, like Jesus Christ. Or a sexy female panther. You have a sleekness and a sureness that drive the mere humans around you insane with desire and envy.

It's irresistible.

For this first NSA Challenge, I want you to decide who you are:

Are you Jesus Christ? Or are you a sexy female panther?

Those are your only two choices.

You may try both, if you'd like.

Either way, you are at ease in all sociosexual situations. You sit at the bar relaxed, needing nothing from the night, because you've spent your day accomplishing things in the desert. You maintain steady eye contact and have amazing posture, knowing that everyone around you wants desperately to reach out and touch your left flank. You expect nothing from the people you meet, because you are better than they are. Either you are being kind and selfless, saying nothing about yourself as you talk to them about their issues and save them from eternal damnation, or you are sitting still, being strong and beautiful, watching them silently and resisting your natural instinct to rip out their intestines.

NSA CHALLENGE

Go to a sociosexual watering hole that you have never visited before, by yourself. This could be a bar, a café with a bar feel to it, or a restaurant with a bar in it. (If you are participating online at NeverSleepAlone.com, take a photo on the way in.)

Have No Expectations.

Sit down. Order a drink from the bartender[1] and give a nice tip[2] with a serene smile. If there are no seats available, resist the temptation to occupy yourself with mind-

---

[1] It is okay if you do not want to drink alcohol. You can order soda, coffee, tea, or even water. Nobody cares what you drink.

[2] Tipping well is very important if you want to Never Sleep Alone. A nice tip creates positive energy, which is easily converted into sexual energy. Do not expect special treatment for your tip! Doing so will give you *The Look of Expectation* and make you seem like an asshole. Be sure you know the tipping customs of whatever country you are in, and always give slightly above the expected. If the bartender gives you something for free, you still tip on whatever the cost of that item would have been. If the bartender gives you a lot of things for free, then the bartender probably wants to sleep with you.

less smartphone games, text messaging, or e-mails. Turn your phone off for a while and accept your right to stand calmly and proudly. Enjoy your surroundings, observe the Mediocre Majority, and truly feel these first moments of your transformation into an Exceptional Individual. Have No Expectations.

Stay at this place for at least an hour and a half. Drink something, eat something,[3] talk to people, if it suits you. Eat and drink slowly, and try to be fully conscious of everything you are seeing, hearing, smelling, tasting, and feeling.

Have No Expectations.

If being fully present initially makes you uncomfortable, resist the urge to turn on your phone. Take out a pen and paper and write a letter to a friend or lover. There is always someone in your life who deserves a nice letter or thank-you note. If anyone asks you what you're doing, smile benevolently and say you are writing a letter to a friend. Enjoy the experience.

---

[3] If you believe you are overweight, do not eat too much food. After completing this challenge go for a walk or run.

Have No Expectations. If you are participating online: When you get home, submit your photo to NeverSleepAlone. com and tell me all about your first NSA Challenge.

NSA Principle 2

BFF = UCB

Best Friend Forever = Ultimate Cock Block

CONGRATULATIONS ON COMPLETING YOUR first NSA Challenge.

I am very proud of you.

By completing your first challenge you have already risen above the Mediocre Majority and taken a major step toward becoming an Exceptional Individual.

Most people will not complete the first challenge.

Most people do not have the courage, confidence, and independence required to go to a sociosexual watering hole alone. Most people go out only with their friends, which is why most people are annoying and unfuckable.

Best Friend Forever = Ultimate Cock Block

If you want to Never Sleep Alone, you must stop going out with your friends.

When same-sex friends go out in a group together, they magnify each other's worst qualities and negate each other's sociosexual power.[1]

Why Women Should Never Go Out in a Group

When women go out in a group together, they talk to each other.

A lot.

And when women talk among themselves, their voices get loud and high-pitched. And the more they talk to each other, the more fun they have with each other, the more cocktails they consume, the LOUDER and HIGHER-

---

[1] Pages 34–43 are meant specifically for heterosexual men and women. Gay, bisexual, lesbian, transgendered, and queer people are sociosexually advanced in these areas and may skip ahead to page 44. Straight men should study gay men to learn how to be well dressed, well groomed, and well mannered. Straight women should study lesbians and the transgendered to learn how to modulate their voice and speak slowly and seductively.

PITCHED their voices become. Eventually, they create a shrill wall of sound that is impossible for the male species to penetrate. And this makes it impossible for a male to desire any of them sexually.

Why?

Men are dogs.

What do all dogs like?

Singular attention, strategic discipline, and banging you from behind.

What do all dogs hate?

High-pitched noises.

What He Hears

Like dogs, all men have instinctual responses to the speed, volume, and tone of the female voice.

When a man hears a woman speaking in a fast, loud, and high-pitched voice, he instinctively feels on guard, because the speed, volume, and tone of her voice instantly make him feel that she is N^3.

N³ = Nagging, Nervous, and Needy

And, like a dog, he will become anxious, and this anxiety will cause him to want to run away from her as quickly as possible.

But when a man hears a woman speaking with a slow, soft, and low-pitched voice, he instinctively feels that she is S³.

S³ = Seductive, Self-Confident, and Sexually Skilled

And, like a dog, he will feel comfortable with this voice, he will want to please this voice, and he will want to hear this voice again. This comfort makes him want to fulfill her desires, follow her home, and sleep curled up next to her.

Therefore, if you are a woman, you must consistently make a conscious effort to keep your volume down and speak slowly in a low-pitched tone.

Always.

Even when you are in a loud place.

Especially when you are in a loud place.

This will make the man have to lean in to you in order to hear you, which not only brings him closer to you but also makes all the other men watching think he wants you.

If *they* think *he* wants you, then *they* will also want you.

And if *he* thinks *they* want you, then *he* will want you even more.

Dogs like to steal from other dogs.

NSA TRUTH

Desire is contagious.

Women: Buy Yourself a "Voice Ring"

Usually, the faster, louder, and higher-pitched a woman talks, the more she talks with her hands. So, if you are a woman, you should buy yourself a beautiful ring to wear on the hand you tend to gesture with the most. Every time you look at that lovely ring, remind yourself to slow down and lower your lovely voice an octave.

DO NOT TELL ANYONE THAT THIS RING IS YOUR "VOICE RING"!

That will make you seem like a psycho.

If anyone asks you about your lovely ring, just smile calmly and say slowly, gently, and in a low-pitched voice, "It was a gift."

Remember, women:

When you are out all alone, you are attractive, adventurous, and alluring.

When you are out with "the girls," you are annoying.

Why Men Should Never Go Out in a Group

In the beginning, all men were gay. Yes, men got married and had wives and children, but they also always had one or more male lovers. Men may find this hard to admit, but females know this to be true because we paid attention in humanities class.

Because of this historical truth, most modern men have repressed homosexual tendencies. And these repressed homosexual tendencies become evident when men go out drinking together.

Men may think that going out in a group to "hang out with your bros" and "pick up chicks" is a good thing. But when a woman sees a group of men out together, something rooted deep within her DNA makes her wonder, "Are those men gay?"

When men go out in a group together, they tend to behave in one of two ways:

1. They Act Like Dogs

They embrace their canine tendencies and go into pack mode, with the alpha dog attempting to lead the pack while the beta males all crowd around him, barking and mimicking him, in a pathetic competition for sociosexual dominance, thus cock-blocking the alpha dog.

Because the alpha dog is drunk, he abandons his role as leader and assimilates into the pack. Then, as a pack, they single out one female and surround her, each competing for her singular attention. They shower her with compliments, fight over her, and buy her drinks, while ignoring her friends. They repeatedly attempt to convince her to abandon her female group and leave with the male pack, thus alienating her from her friends and making her feel like a cheap hooker at a beta-male bachelor party.

Or:

2. They Act Gay

They embrace their homosexual tendencies and also become ridiculously immature and embarrassingly cheap.

Usually, they completely ignore the women around them and engross themselves in juvenile homoerotic rituals such as billiards, foosball, or low-stakes poker. Sometimes, in an effort to prove their male solidarity, they will annoy and insult the women around them and often engage nearby females in inane nonsexual conversations, without offering them drinks.

What She Sees

Therefore, when a female sees a group of men out together, her primitive instincts kick in, and she immediately sees either a pack of beta dogs who are not worthy of her attention or a pack of gay men who would rather swap movie quotes and do shots off each other's dicks than buy her a drink and receive a nice heterosexual blow job.

Even when a male who is evolutionarily advanced decides to break off from the canine-homo pack, approach a woman, and make a genuine attempt at a sociosexual connection, it's too late, because her defenses are already up.

She instinctually feels that he is insulting her intelligence, and in an effort to maintain her dignity, she will reject his advances.

But when a woman sees a man out all by himself, confidently standing at a bar all alone, she automatically sees him as the one alpha who can save her from drowning in a sea of beta-male douchebags and she will welcome any interaction with him.

Remember, men:

When you are out alone, you act like a real man who wants to put his real penis inside a real woman's vagina.

When you are out with "the bros," you act like a gay dog.

Men: Offer Her a Drink

If you find a woman at a bar sexually attractive, you can accelerate interactions with her by offering her a drink. If you are at a crowded sociosexual watering hole, a good technique is to squeeze into a spot that is next to an attractive woman. Right before or right after you get the bartender's attention, turn to the woman and say, "I'm ordering a drink. Can I offer you one?"

You should *never* expect anything in return for buying a woman a drink. You are doing it because you are a generous human being.

Perhaps you don't have a lot of money?

That's great!

For every drink you buy a woman, that's one less drink that you can afford to buy for yourself, which is usually a good thing. Most men tend to drink way more than they should, which leads to bad breath, bad behavior, belly fat, and whiskey dick.

You Talk in Questions?

When you are making a declarative *statement*, you tend to place emphasis at the end of each *phrase*, as though you are asking a *question*? When you're not actually asking a *question*? This makes you sound rather stupid and very *insecure*? This gets much worse when you're out with a group of your same-sex *friends*? Because same-sex friends unconsciously mimic each other's *speech patterns*? This is making you *unfuckable*? You need to stop doing this *immediately*?

Yes.

Stop it.

Sociosexual Sabotage

Human beings are naturally competitive for sociosexual attention. This competiveness is rooted deep within our DNA, so your friends can't help but be jealous when you are the only one getting attention.

This instinctive jealousy will cause your friends to sabotage your potential NSA hookups, EFT.

Every
Fucking
Time

Your friends are not bad people. Often, they do not consciously realize they are ruining things for you, and sometimes, their well-intentioned efforts to try to *help* you hook up will have the opposite effect, and instead make you look desperate and sexually irrelevant.

The most common way this happens is when your friend says something stupid to or near the person you are hoping to seduce. Something that your friend *thinks* will make you look cool but that actually makes you look like a desperate and mediocre loser.

Examples:

"He's the nicest guy I know."

"She makes a lot of money."

"He's a really good dad."

"If you hurt her, I will kill you. She's, like, my family, and she tells me everything."

"He would never tell you this, but he really likes you."

"I want her to find a good guy. She's been so slutty lately."

"Bro, the bartender's saying your credit card was declined."

"Oh, did the doctor ever call you about your results?"

NSA TRUTH

Your best friends are your worst sexual enemies.

Always Have a Mission

If you are anxious about going out by yourself at first, just make sure to always have a mission when you go out. A mission is something you want to accomplish while you are out in public. This could be reading a book, editing a colleague's résumé, studying a foreign language, or writing a letter to a friend or lover.

Most people complain of being "bored" or "uncomfortable" when they go out alone. That's why you see people drinking too much and anxiously looking at their cell phones all the time.

You are better than those mediocre people.

You never drink too much and you never look at your phone, because you always have something important to do. Therefore you have no reason to be anxious and no time to have expectations.

You are at that bar because you have something you *want* to do, and you want to do it at that bar. This combination of purpose and desire is very attractive. You will find that the more focused you are on your mission, the more people will be drawn to you.

I highly recommend writing letters as your mission. You can write to me or to one of your friends, lovers, or colleagues. You can send postcards, thank-you notes, invitations to a dinner party at your house, etc. Writing letters is a great way to improve your communication skills, reflect on your newfound knowledge and power, and make friends and lovers feel special while enhancing your *Aura of Experience*.

Do *not* write on a computer or electronic device like the other mediocre people in the room do. When you are out in public, do the opposite of the Mediocre Majority.

Be sensual and unique by actually putting pen to paper.

I always write on paper when I go out alone.

And I Never Sleep Alone.

Unless I want to.

This Is *Your* NSA Journey

NSA is about being open to new people and new experiences. You must have the freedom to say yes to every new experience that you want to have. When you're out with your friends, you have to take their desires into consideration, and you can't always say yes when you want to.

NSA is about living life with No Expectations. It is impossible to do this with your friends around, because they come with their own expectations. They expect you to be considerate of their desires, they expect you to behave in a certain way, and they expect you to play the same mediocre and sexually irrelevant role you have always played within that social group.

NSA is about you fearlessly reinventing yourself whenever you want, until you find what works for you. You must feel free to play with different personas and experiment with different sociosexual roles so that you can become the most beautiful and powerful version of yourself.

If your friends are around, you will feel very self-conscious exploring and experimenting, you will never live up to your full sociosexual potential, and you will never discover who you truly are.

You are capable of being the sexiest and most powerful person in the world.

But you must do this on your own.

You want to become The One. . .

The One stands alone.

NSA CHALLENGE

Close your eyes and visualize a romantic and exotic foreign country that you have always wanted to visit.

In what faraway land do you see yourself eating the most delicious meals of your life, partying with the locals late into the night, taking up temporary residence in an architectural masterpiece, and making passionate love to a magnificent stranger as the dawn breaks over the horizon?

Get dressed in an outfit that makes you feel beautiful and powerful when you look in the mirror.

Then go to a bookstore alone and buy a travel guide for that magical place you have never been. Take your new travel book, along with pen and paper, to a lively sociosexual watering hole that serves delicious food.

Do not invite any of your friends to meet you.

Take a seat at the bar,[2] turn off your phone, and enjoy a long and leisurely meal alone while you read your travel book and begin planning your dream trip.

You *will* be going on this trip by yourself within the next six months. And you will be visiting at least one foreign country every year for the rest of your life. Solo international travel is essential to being an Exceptional Individual. Don't worry if you don't have the money[3] yet or if you think it will be difficult to take time off.

Stop making excuses and start making an itinerary.

You will find that once you begin clearly articulating your desires and creating a step-by-step plan, everything and everyone around you will conspire to make your fantasy a reality.

If anyone asks you what you are doing, say: "I'm plan-

---

[2] If you want to meet new people and have new experiences, you must always choose restaurants that have lively bar scenes and you must always take your meals at the bar.

[3] Solo international travel is easier and less expensive than you think. Visit NeverSleepAlone.com for tips on how to make your NSA travel dreams come true.

ning a trip to _____." If they ask you *why* you are going to this amazing location all by yourself, smile and say: "Because I want to."

If participating online at NeverSleepAlone.com, submit your dream itinerary. The sexiest and most inspired itineraries will be entered to win a free vacation anywhere in the world the winner wants to go.

NSA Principle 3

STAR

Style Transcends Actual Reality

BY CHANGING THE WAY you look, the way you live, and the way you love, you can transcend your former self and create a beautiful new existence that you will love inhabiting and that everyone you meet will want to inhabit with you.

Most people lead uninspired and unsatisfying lives.

They never take risks, they seldom travel, and they fear change. That's why most people like watching movies about adventurous archaeologists or suburban housewives who leave everything behind to travel around the world, eating everything and fucking everyone.

Deep down, people *want* to take risks, people *want* to travel, people *want* to have Mind-Blowing Orgasms with mysterious strangers in cinematic locations.

But they never will.

They will never explore ancient tombs in Egypt or rescue unique beauties in Nepal. They will never ride bicycles through wine country or have picnics by the river. They will never make sweet love in a secret garden on the outskirts of Paris as the spring sun warms their naked back and their perfect lover gazes dreamily into their eyes and asks, "Why are you so amazing?"

Instead, they will waste their lives staring glassy-eyed at a screen, impotent voyeurs of the exciting and romantic life they will never lead.

But YOU are better than the fearful, unimaginative, and lazy Mediocre Majority.

You are a bold and creative Exceptional Individual who is no longer going to waste the precious time you have left on this planet watching movies and wishing your life were different. From this point forward, you are going to . . .

BE THE MOVIE

If you want to Never Sleep Alone, you must realize that your life is an exciting and romantic movie that the whole world is watching.

YOU are the star of this movie.

When you are the star of your own movie, you inspire and seduce everyone around you by making them feel as though *they* are living in a movie. Your unique appearance, your heightened presence, your adventurous lifestyle, and the sensual atmosphere you create give the people you interact with the same rush of euphoria they feel when they are watching a movie they love.

They will become addicted to this feeling, which will make them become addicted to YOU.

Style
Transcends
Actual
Reality

Dress and carry yourself in a way that heightens your presence and incites passionate reactions from others. Live in an exquisite environment that inspires you and awakens the senses of everyone who enters your home.

Constantly be creating something that is very important to you.

And never allow your passion for another person to eclipse your passion for your own life.

The Way You Look

Do you want to sleep with either of these people?

Neither do I.

My genitals recoil at the sight of these wretched creatures.

How many times this month have you left the house looking like that?

How many times have you unwittingly broadcast to the world: "I'm undersexed, I'm overworked, I'm on a strict budget, and I live an uninspired life"?

Why would you do that, when with a little imagination and a few minutes effort, you could easily look like this . . .

These people are stars.

We want to be in their movie.

We want to be just like them and we want to sleep with them.

Clothing vs. Costumes

The people in the first photo are wearing clothing. Clothing is meant to cover nudity and protect human beings from the elements.

Boring.

Mediocre.

When you are wearing clothing and someone looks at you, they feel nothing.

The people in the second photo are wearing *costumes*. Costumes reveal a bit about you while suggesting a greater story and arousing the senses and emotions of everyone who looks at you.

You stir their imagination.

You make them want to know your story.

You make them want to be in your movie.

You should never go anywhere unless you are wearing a costume that makes you feel beautiful and powerful and arouses the *curiosity* and *desire* of everyone who looks at you.

NSA TRUTH

Curiosity and desire are the foundations
of sexual attraction and romantic obsession.

Costumes don't have to be overly elaborate. They can be very simple. The important things are:

1. You *think* about who you want to be.

2. You *create* a costume that reinforces this image of yourself, while intriguing others into wanting to know more about you.

Curiosity and desire.

You must also put thought into what you wear when you're home alone, because who you are in private is just as important as who you are in public.

Ask yourself, "Am I a sexually irrelevant and depressed person in faded sweatpants, mismatched socks, and a coffee-stained Pearl Jam T-shirt? Or am I an adventurous, sensual, and sexually powerful person in black silk pajamas?"

I'm often asked: "But what kinds of costumes should I wear?"

When creating your costumes, you have two options:

1. Your first option is to appropriate the style of one of your favorite characters from a work of art. Recall one of your favorite movies, favorite books, or favorite paintings, and identify the character who compelled you the most in this work of art.

Who is the character you most want to be like?

Who is the character that all the other characters want to sleep with?

If you love classic films, this may be Holly Golightly from *Breakfast at Tiffany's* or James Bond from *Goldfinger*. If you are literary, this may be Lady Brett Ashley from *The Sun Also Rises* or Aragorn from *The Lord of the Rings*. If you love fine art, this may be Max Kurzweil's *The Lady in the Yellow Dress* or the fisherman in Frederic Leighton's *The Fisherman and the Syren*.

Now think about that character's *style*.

Think about the way that character looks, the way that character lives, and the way that character loves. Use that character as a template and feel free to modify the image to fit your desires. When you are out in the world, living your life and completing your NSA Challenges, imagine that you are as unique and provocative as the character that inspired your image.

Curiosity and desire.

2. Your other option is to costume yourself according to the Collective Erotic Unconscious and embody a sociosexual archetype. The Collective Erotic Unconscious embodies mankind's universal experiences of the primeval emotions of love, lust, envy, and fear. Sociosexual archetypes are the characters who have recurred throughout history in various forms, stirring within us those prime-

val emotions, while simultaneously representing our own inner struggle between light and dark.

I know it seems complicated, but all you really need to understand is that every woman on earth wants to sleep with a sensitive soldier, an intelligent investment banker, a masculine dance instructor, or a rich vampire.

And every man on earth wants to sleep with a prostitute in a red dress, his mother in a flowing gown, or his best friend in a tailored suit.

Accept these undeniable truths.

Then costume yourself and behave accordingly.

Costumes don't have to be expensive. You can usually create a romantic and inspiring costume for a fraction of the cost of the boring clothing you usually wear.

Clothing is about function.

Costumes are about fantasy.

Make it your goal to be a walking fantasy.

Curiosity and desire.

And remember, the way you smell is even more important than the way you look. Never smell like dying flowers, mothballs, creamed corn, aged cheese, stale beer, a musty attic, an abandoned butcher shop, or an active fishing boat. If you use perfume or cologne, invest in quality scents and remember that a little goes a long way. Make sure the clothes you wear have been recently cleaned, especially if they are vintage.

Shower daily, never forgetting to clean your ears, nails, and belly button every time.

Brush your teeth and floss at least twice a day. Use gum or mints after smoking or drinking coffee or alcohol, and visit the dentist regularly so that your mouth doesn't smell like a rotting corpse.

NSA TRUTH

Bad breath is the number-one killer of seduction.

Never Sleep Alone

Make sure your hair and armpits always smell like heaven and your genitals always taste like ambrosia.

Eat lots of pineapple.

Avoid asparagus.

The Importance of Sunglasses

Wear sunglasses.

Every day.

Rain or shine.[1]

A nice pair of sunglasses will instantly make you look attractive, adventurous, and effortlessly elegant. Dark sunglasses also allow you to look at whomever you want whenever you want, without people knowing you are looking at them. This automatically improves your posture and raises your confidence, placing you well above the Mediocre Majority.

Also, because people can't see your eyes, their minds

---

[1] Do not wear sunglasses at night. Doing so will give you *The Look of Expectation* and make you seem like an asshole.

trick them into believing that *you* can't see *their* eyes, even though they are *not* wearing sunglasses. They forget themselves and stare at you openly. It's amazing.

Start wearing sunglasses every day and you will see that I am right about this. No matter how sunny or cloudy or hot or cold it is outside.

Wear sunglasses.

And watch them watch you.

Possessions vs. Props

The mediocre people in the photo on page 60 are weighed down by their possessions. Their shit. The same boring shit most people carry around with them on a daily basis, i.e., cell phones, computers, disposable coffee cups, children.

The Exceptional Individuals in the photo on page 62 have *props*. Props are unique and inspiring items that enhance your costume and intrigue people into wanting to know more about you.

One look at these exceptional stars with their beautiful

costumes and intriguing props, and we begin to feel that strange mix of curiosity and desire as we imagine all sorts of things about them and their exciting lives. We think he might be a traveling photographer or a sexually dominant architect. We think she might be an actress or a gallery owner or a young French widow.

We want to know their stories, we want to be in their movie, we want to be just like them, and we want to sleep with them because we find them very attractive.

You are very attractive.

Being attractive has nothing to do with being classically beautiful. Being attractive means you take care in your appearance and your environment, you always have an interesting story to share, and you exhibit *at least one quality* that makes you unique and draws people to you.

Think about your best attributes, enhance them, and put them on display for the world to see.

For instance, if you are a man with bright and penetrating eyes, when indoors, you should never hide your eyes with prescription glasses. Get contacts and wear them every time you are out in public. Or, if you are a good candidate, get laser vision correction. And if you like wearing a suit, wear a suit or suit jacket whenever possible. A suit jacket will instantly improve your posture while enhancing your manly physique, and you do not need a special occasion to wear one. Women love men in suit jackets.

If you are a woman with very nice breasts, you should go braless whenever possible and wherever appropriate. Get some thin and elegantly cut silky shirts and low-backed dresses and wear them with confidence. Men lose their minds for a classy and intelligent woman who decides she doesn't need to wear a bra.

If you are a man who has all his hair, get a good stylist to give you an interesting and attractive haircut. If you are a woman who has beautiful feet, always have beautifully painted and exposed toes. Most women love nice hair and most men have foot fetishes.

Costumes and props are essential to being attractive, and they help accelerate your social interactions, because most people are shy and awkward.

Most people need an excuse to approach you, and they need a reason to feel comfortable continuing a conversation with you. Make it easy for them by exhibiting unique qualities, wearing an inspiring costume, and carrying intriguing props that make people want to know your story.

Imagine that your life is now a romantic and exciting movie. Imagine that you are the star of this movie and you must completely immerse yourself in your new character and fully embody the sexy, inspiring, and powerful role you are now playing. Think about who you are, what turns you on in life, and what you want people to feel the second they lay eyes on you.

Think about what costumes you can wear and what kinds of props you can carry that will enhance the image you are trying to project and intrigue sexy strangers into wanting to know more about you.

Devote this week to creating a few ideal, romantic costumes and acquiring intriguing props. Look around your house for interesting pieces you may have forgotten. Go out to department stores, boutiques, thrift stores, and flea markets and find the things that will make your fantasy a reality.

Don't forget to get a pair of nice sunglasses.

Make this promise to yourself and keep it: "I will never go out in public unless I look and feel like the star of my own movie."

The Way You Live

As a star, your job is to inspire and seduce everyone around you into wanting to become a part of your world. Your home is the most important part of that world. You must be inspired and turned on by your own environment. The second someone walks through your door, they must feel like they are entering the magical, sensual world of an Exceptional Individual.

Therefore, you must eliminate all of the nonsensual shit that most people usually have in their homes and create a unique and exquisite environment that is cinematically beautiful and appeals to the five senses of sight, smell, sound, taste, and touch.

Curiosity and desire.

You Must Eliminate This
Shit from Your Home

If you want to Never Sleep Alone, whether you are a male or a female, you must immediately and permanently eliminate the following nonsensual shit from your home:

Dirty Laundry, Dirty Dishes, Dirty Litter Boxes, Dirty Pets, [2] ***Dirty Anything:*** It's gross. Clean it, hide it, or throw it away. Keep your home clean, tidy, and smelling amazing at all times. Do not be like the Mediocre Majority. Never have shoes by the door, unopened mail on the table, or a "junk bowl" with keys, credit cards, prescription bottles, and other non-sensual shit. Have beautiful, lidded boxes and a closet or storage space where you can throw things until

---

[2] Keep your pets off your bed and out of your bedroom at all times. They are worse cock blockers than your BFFs.

you have time to put them in their proper places. Never leave your home unless it is clean and tidy. You never know if you'll be bringing someone back with you.

If you believe you are too busy to keep your house clean, hire a cleaning person. It's not that expensive. If you really can't afford to hire someone, there are a lot of people with slave fetishes who will gladly clean your house and do your errands for free and expect nothing in return.

Over the years, I've had seven great slaves and I have never once been asked to touch their genitals. I did once beat a slave with a broom, but only because he begged me. He had been cleaning my grout with a toothbrush for three days straight.

Fluorescent Lighting: It makes everyone look horrible and feel gross. Overhead lighting of any kind is a bad idea. Get a few floor lamps and table lamps and make sure you have soft lightbulbs and dimmer switches on all light sources. Your movie needs to be lit well.

Plastic Dishes, Plastic Utensils, and Plastic Containers of Anything: Never eat off plastic plates or drink out of plastic glasses. Plastic is the nonsensual material of choice for preschools and insane asylums. If you buy products that come in plastic, either hide them in a cupboard or throw the plastic away and put the items in pretty bowls and jars on the counter and in your refrigerator. Always serve water and juice in a glass or ceramic pitcher.

Magazines, Newspapers, or Books in the Bathroom: Nobody wants to think of you reading on the toilet.

Photos of Exes, Photos of You When You Were Much Younger, Photos of Dead Pets: These imply that you are holding on to the past, which is very depressing and very unattractive. And don't display your graduation photos. No matter how recent it was, it's just sad to think you're still holding on to that day. Get a new high point.

"Collections" of Anything: Collections imply an obsessive personality, which is very unattractive. You are a star. You don't have singular obsessions; you have many passions. Sell that collection and buy some new costumes and props.

Sports Posters or Paraphernalia: You are not a fan.

You're a player. Replace that baseball card collection with an actual baseball and bat.

Stuffed Animals, Toys, Dolls, or Action Figures: Grow up.

Essentials for an Exquisite Environment

If you want to Never Sleep Alone, whether you are a male or a female, you must have the essential elements and items listed below in your home:

Candles: Candles instantly transform the appearance of a home and create a warm and sensual environment. Candlelight is also the most flattering light for the human face and body. You must have lots of unscented candles of various sizes all over your home. Avoid candles that are in the shape of animals, flowers, or anything else ridiculous. Stick to simple tapers, pillars, votives, and tea lights.

When you invite someone over at night, turn on one dim lamp and then ask the person to light candles for you while you get them something to drink, turn on music, and change into something more comfortable. Asking your guest to light candles for you or with you will heighten their senses and put them at ease.

You should also have a few scented candles around, but make sure they are all the same scent and make sure to choose seductive scents that are spice or citrus based. Don't have more than two in a room as the scent will be overpowering. Avoid floral scents and candles that smell like baked goods, as those will make people think of a grandparent or ex-wife.

Music: Your life is a movie and the best movies have memorable sound tracks. You should always have at least three hours of diverse, inspiring, and sensual music ready to play the second you arrive home. Keep a stack of your favorite CDs or records by your stereo system or create an NSA playlist on your computer or mobile device.

Check out NeverSleepAlone.com to stream some of my NSA playlists.

Always play music through a decent set of speakers or a stereo system. Computer sound is depressing.

Put the music on the second you walk in the door. Better yet, keep it playing while you're gone so that whenever you enter your home, the sound track of your movie is always playing. Even when home alone, you should make listening to beautiful and inspiring music a part of your daily existence.

Champagne, Wine, Basic Liquors, and Nonalcoholic Beverages: Keep your home stocked with several good options.

Fresh Flowers and Live Plants: One bouquet of fresh flowers instantly transforms an ordinary room into a romantic and cinematic environment. Live plants not only make your home more interesting, they fill your home with extra oxygen, which turns people on.

Never have dying flowers or plants in your house. No dried flowers, either. Dried flowers are the decoration of choice for suicidal teenagers and bitter old women. They will make people unconsciously think of dying animals and decaying genitalia.

Avoid fake plants and plastic flowers. It's your home, not a Chinese restaurant.

A Bowl of Fresh Fruit: Always keep a bowl of real fresh fruit on your kitchen table or counter. Looking at fruit makes people think about oral sex. Eating fruit (especially pineapple!) makes people's genitals taste amazing.

If you don't know what fruit to buy to make an aesthetically pleasing fruit bowl, think PABLO: pears, apples, bananas, lemons, oranges.

And also include a pineapple, whenever possible.

Interesting Art: You can buy art, or make your own paintings or sculptures. You can also blow up beautiful photos you have taken of places you have been or places you want to go.

Quality Towels and Sheets: Always have soft, clean sheets on your beautifully made bed. Never have faded, torn, or stained bedding, as these will make people think of homeless shelters and hospice care. Have a woven basket of clean, rolled-up, white towels in the bathroom.

This will make people want to take a shower with you.

Coffee and Tea: Most people want coffee or tea in the morning. You must have these on hand in case someone spends the night.

Extra Toothbrushes: Because using a finger as a toothbrush is unsanitary and depressing.

Condoms: Self-explanatory.

Dedicate the next week to cleaning your house from top to bottom, acquiring the essentials for an exquisite home, and transforming your living space into a cinematic and inspiring environment.

The Way You Love

You should feel 100 percent comfortable loving everybody you want to love.

NSA TRUTH

Give love freely to everybody and nobody will ever feel threatened by it.

But remember, love is very different from obsession. When you are obsessed with somebody, you *expect* something from that person. But when you *love* somebody, you simply seek to make that person happy while expecting nothing in return.

The only person you are allowed to be obsessed with is yourself. And, from now on, you must constantly be creating something that is very important to YOU.

All human beings have an inherent internal need to create. Most people are too lazy or too scared to bring their creative ideas to fruition. And it is the denial and suppression of the personal creative urge that makes people become obsessed with other human beings.

You will notice that throughout history, artists have always been the most seductive and sexually powerful people. Because artists are constantly creating something that is very important to them, they are completely obsessed with their own world, so they do not become obsessed with other people.

Other people become obsessed with them.

You are an artist.

You have many creative ideas in your head, from trying a new recipe, to writing a novel, to painting your bathroom wall.

Your past obsessions with other human beings were simply your inherent creative need having no other outlet. Therefore in order to become confident, fulfilled, and supremely attractive to everyone you meet, you must begin to actively work on these ideas and make daily creation your top priority.

You must paint the wall, take the acting class, learn the guitar, cook the homemade pasta, write the epic poem, make the pornographic sock puppets—whatever creative idea you have in your head, you must make it your first priority to dedicate as much time as possible every day to bringing that creative idea to life.

Even if you can devote only ten minutes a day to working on your creations, it is essential that you make the time to do it. Constant creation will prevent you from becoming obsessed with anyone or anything but yourself and the world you are constantly creating.

This potent combination of universal love, self-obsession, and constant creativity is devastatingly attractive to people. Everyone you meet will be envious of the way you live your life and they will want to become a part of your world.

People will soon start to say to you, "Your life is like a movie!"

And soon after that, they will all want to be given a part in your movie.

Curiosity and desire.

Your Supporting Cast

You must begin to think of every sexually relevant person you meet as a potential member of your supporting cast, and nothing more.

YOU are the star of your own movie. *You* decide who you are going to let into your movie and *you* decide how big or small their role will be. When you interact with these people, you do it without effort or anxiety, because you are not trying to prove yourself to anyone. *You* are the star. They are just potential members of your supporting cast. *They* have to prove themselves to *you*.

If it helps, you can think of your interactions with members of the opposite sex as scenes where they are auditioning for you.

But, because you are a generous and confident star, you give *every* scene and *every* potential cast member all of your focus and energy, doing your best to make them feel like stars too. Though you do not get overly emotionally invested, you always do your best to make every potential cast member feel amazing and have a magical time with you, because you know this may be the only chance they get to be in a movie with someone of your caliber.

NSA CHALLENGE

Begin planning a simple and elegant dinner party that will happen at your home two weeks from now. As a star, you will now be having dinner parties every two weeks. Your dinner party can be an elaborate three-course meal, a simple party where you make one pasta dish or order delicious takeout and serve it on beautiful dishes, or a wine and cheese party, where every guest brings a bottle of wine and exotic cheese—whatever your mood and budget dictate. The important thing is that your home be an exquisite environment, that you play inspiring music throughout the party, that you have lots of candles burning, and that you wear an intriguing and inspiring costume.

Your dinner parties should always have between four and twelve guests total, including yourself, and, whenever possible, have an equal number of males and females.

Do not invite any of your existing friends to your

first dinner party. Eventually, you can invite your existing friends, but not now. You will be meeting lots of new people in the next two weeks while completing your NSA Challenges and these are the people you will invite.

When inviting people to your dinner party, say, "I'm having a dinner party on _____. I'd love it if you could come." If anyone asks *why* you are having a dinner party, say, "Oh, I always throw dinner parties. Getting interesting people together over an amazing meal is one of my favorite things in life. You're very interesting, so I do hope you can join the group. How shall I send your invitation?"

Tell them you need their RSVP by three days before the party so you know how much food to prepare.

Have your party and have No Expectations.

Two weeks after your first dinner party, have another dinner party.

Repeat forever throughout your life.

Be sure to send me photos of your dinner parties at NeverSleepAlone.com. If they incite my curiosity and desire, perhaps I'll invite you to a dinner party at my house.

NSA Principle 4

FIRE

Fearless, Independent, Relaxed, Erotic

IF YOU WANT TO Never Sleep Alone, you must be:

> **F**earless
> **I**ndependent
> **R**elaxed
> **E**rotic

These are the four most attractive qualities in a human being.

Most people are lacking in one or all of these areas. So if you can attain these four qualities and make your FIRE burn brightly, you will immediately be better than most people, which will make most people want to sleep with you.

We are going to talk about each of these four qualities in detail. Then I am going to tell you the 3 Things You Must

Do in order to attain these qualities, make your FIRE burn brightly, and instantly accelerate your transformation into The One.

Then you are going to actually do them.

You Are Fearless

Most people are not fearless.

Most people are scared of everything.

They are scared of heights, or they are scared of clowns, or they are scared to be alone, or they are scared they are going to die.

Here is something you must understand:

You *are* going to die.

Say it.

"I am going to die."

You are going to die.

And, unless you are lucky enough to die instantly in an accident, you are probably going to spend a long time dying. There are going to be days, months, years, maybe

even decades when you are unhealthy, weak, sexually irrelevant, and unable to do the things you always wanted to do.
Therefore, the only thing to be scared of is wasting the best
years of your life not living the life you want, all because of
your fears.

Usually, your fears are not even your own. Most of
your fears have been unconsciously inherited from others.
For instance, nobody who *says* they are scared of clowns
is actually scared of clowns. They *say* they are scared of
clowns only because they heard *other people* saying they
were scared of clowns. If somebody was actually scared of
clowns, they would never say so. Because just talking about
the clowns would make them pee on the floor.

Sometimes, your fears come from a past trauma.
Maybe a clown actually did something very bad to you or a
loved one. If that is the case, you must get serious help to
overcome this past trauma.

Oftentimes, you are fearful because you have tried
something only one time, and the first time you tried it, you
had an undesirable reaction. Maybe the first time you saw

a clown, you actually did pee on the floor, and this one bad reaction has kept you from going to the circus ever again.

You must identify your fears and decide if they are inherited fears or actual fears. Once you've identified them, you must face these fears and get over them.

If it's an inherited fear, then simply forget about it.

Right now.

Do you really want to be another one of those annoying people who falsely claim to be scared of clowns? If it's an actual fear that stems from a serious trauma, get serious help.

Right now.

You don't want to let something that happened in the past continue to ruin your present beautiful existence.

If it is a fear that stems from having a bad reaction the first time you tried something new, then you must try it again and again and again until you are over it. Pay a clown to perform a private show at your house, put down a plastic tarp, and pee all over the place until you are finally over it.

The only way to eliminate fear is to face it.

By completing the first three NSA Challenges, you have already faced people's most common fears and gotten over them. You are well on your way to becoming fearless. Whenever you feel fear, identify it, face it, and immediately take steps to get over it.

NSA TRUTH

The only way to get over it is to get over it.

You Are Independent

Most people are not independent.

Most people are extremely dependent on the opinions and desires of other people and most people are extremely dependent on technology. Most people put the opinions and desires of friends, lovers, family, and society before their own.

Most people rarely experience anything alone, without constantly looking at their phone or updating their Facebook wall.

If you have been fully actualizing the first three NSA Principles and have completed all of the NSA Challenges up to this point, you are already well on your way to becoming completely independent. You already recognize the power of going out alone and avoiding the constant use of technology. You are already spending most of your time doing what *you* want to do, when *you* want to do it, without worrying about what anybody else is thinking or doing.

I am very proud of you.

Keep it up.

It really turns me on.

You Are Relaxed

Most people are not relaxed.

Because most people have a shortage of new experiences and a surplus of expectations and because most people do not know how to put their energy to good use, most people are tense, anxious, or overexcited, and this gives them *The Look of Expectation*, which, as we have discussed, is really gross.

You have been putting your energy to good use lately. You have been increasing your experiences and decreasing your expectations. You are already much more relaxed now than when you began reading this book. Once you begin actualizing this NSA Principle and start doing the 3 Things You Must Do on a regular basis, you are going to be fully relaxed at all times.

You Are Erotic

Most people are not erotic.

Being erotic means combining sensuality and sexuality to arouse intense feelings of desire in yourself and other people.

The erotic force is the most powerful force in the universe. It is a force that people are simultaneously drawn to and scared of. You will notice that every major work of art, entertainment, or advertisement that is created for public consumption is extremely erotic. You look at it and it provokes a feeling of desire within you. You will also notice that the most memorable public figures of all time—Cleopatra, Pablo Picasso, Elvis, Marilyn Monroe, JFK—embraced the erotic side of themselves and capitalized on the suppressed eroticism of others.

Most people either are afraid to be erotic or do not know how to be erotic.

You are better than those mediocre people.

You have been erotic for pages.

You pay attention to the way things look, sound, feel, smell, and taste. You understand that by appealing to the senses, you incite sexual desire in everyone who meets you. You understand the immense power of sexual desire. You do not deny the erotic side of yourself, you openly express your erotic nature, and you encourage others around you to openly express their erotic natures.

FIRE: The 3 Things You Must Do

In order to fully become Fearless, Independent, Relaxed, and Erotic, you must know the 3 Things You Must Do. And you must strive to actually do these things every day. It will be difficult. There may be a day when you don't want to do the 3 Things You Must Do.

But you must.

Everybody is fully capable of doing these things every day of their lives. But most people never do. So, if you can actually do the 3 Things You Must Do consistently, you will be better than most people, which will make most people want to sleep with you.

Are you ready?

We will begin with the easiest and conclude with the most difficult.

Dr. Alex Schiller

1. You must have Mind-Blowing Orgasms.

In order to be Fearless, Independent, Relaxed, and Erotic, you must have MBOs on a regular basis. If you are not orgasmically satisfied, you will walk around with *The Look of Expectation* on your face, which, as we have discussed, is really damn gross.

I highly suggest having MBOs with other people as often as you'd like. But in order for you to be able to receive MBOs from other people, you must first know how to give yourself an MBO whenever you want one. The only way to become proficient at having MBOs is to practice, practice, practice. You must embrace masturbation as a good thing and make it an active part of your life.

You must do it.

You can use your imagination, pornography, toys, other people—anything you want that helps you achieve orgasm. It may be difficult at first, but I promise, with consistent practice you will learn how to achieve an MBO whenever you want one.

I suggest limiting yourself to less than an hour a day of masturbation, because if you go over an hour a day, you will begin to feel guilty and you will have less time to have new experiences and meet new people who want to sleep with you and give you MBOs.

Having MBOs on a regular basis is absolutely essential for your physical appearance, mental stability, and emotional well-being.

2. *You Must Exercise Often*

Exercise means exerting your body in a focused manner for an extended period of time. Yes, it is difficult. If it is not difficult, it is not exercise. And if you do not exercise consistently and constantly challenge yourself to get to the next level of fitness, you will not achieve the maximum benefits and you will never become Fearless, Independent, Relaxed, and Erotic.

You must make the time to exercise and you must exercise as often as possible.

If you are not used to exercise, begin with a small commitment of ten minutes a day, three days a week. It *will* make an immediate positive difference to your physical appearance and mental state. You may not see it or feel it at first, but other people will. And very soon, you will too.

You must do it.

Once you have kept that commitment for one week, gradually increase your commitment. Eventually, you want to get to the point where you are exercising for an hour a day, every day.

I don't care if you love your body exactly as it is. You must still exercise. Exercise is not about vanity. Regular exercise is essential to your health and it is essential to being Fearless, Independent, Relaxed, and Erotic. Regardless of age, weight, or body type, every person on earth should strive to exercise for one hour every day. You will find that on the days you make yourself exercise for one hour, the other hours of the day are spent feeling incredibly powerful, extremely relaxed, and undeniably sexy. You will also find that once you begin exercising regularly, your MBOs become much more intense.

With regular exercise, everything looks better, everything sounds better, everything smells better, everything tastes better, everything feels better, everything *is* better.

3. *You Must End Your Dependency on Your Mobile Phone*

Unless you can end your dependency on your mobile phone, you will never be Fearless, Independent, Relaxed, and Erotic and you will never become The One.

You have developed a great fear of living your life without constantly looking at your mobile phone. Your phone has made you very dependent on the opinions and approval of others because it enables and encourages you to virtually consult outside sources instead of making a choice for yourself.

Your phone does not allow you to ever be fully relaxed because it has created an anxious need in you to be in constant virtual communication via text messages, e-mails, Facebook, and other social media outlets.

Your smartphone is severely diminishing your erotic energy, because when you are connected to your phone, you are incapable of fully connecting to the real world, sensing erotic vibrations from other human beings, and truly experiencing your existence.

Mobile phones are turning human beings into sociosexually retarded robots who are awkward, desperate, and nearly incapable of making true human connections. The next time you are out, look around you at all of the mediocre people who are staring at their phones with *The Look of Expectation* on their faces.

You do not want to be one of those people.

Your phone is also robbing you of anywhere from two to six hours a day of your existence because it is enabling and encouraging you to waste hours of time in nonessential communication with your friends, family, and other sexually irrelevant people. You must start living without your mobile phone as often as possible. You must get into the habit of turning it off and leaving it at home.

You must do it.

Don't say: "But what if someone is trying to get ahold of me?!"

People can wait.

People want to wait.

You must learn to make people wait.

NSA TRUTH

Making people wait makes people
want to sleep with you.

Curiosity and desire.

Even if you truly need your phone for work, you can still turn it off and leave it at home for certain periods of time. Begin by making a rule that you will keep your phone turned off for the last hour before you go to bed at night and for the first hour when you wake up in the morning.

Then make a commitment to leave it at home when you go out at night at least one night a week. You must then learn to turn it off and/or leave it at home when you eat, when you exercise, when you engage in conversations with people, when you masturbate, when you have sex, and whenever possible, for as long as possible.

If you can do this, you will immediately begin to feel your life changing for the better and your FIRE will begin to burn stronger than ever. You will immediately begin to notice how much more time you have in a day to have new experiences, meet new people, and have MBOs. You will eventually begin to feel like the most confident and attractive person in every sociosexual situation.

Those are the 3 Things You Must Do.

I guarantee you that if you can actually make yourself do them consistently, you will become Fearless, Independent, Relaxed, and Erotic and everyone you meet will want to sleep with you.

If you can actually begin to do these things, and keep doing them on a regular basis, you will become The One.

If you don't, you won't.

On your next day off, begin your day by having one or more MBOs, either by having sex with another human being or by masturbating. Make sure that your phone is turned off before you begin and keep it off until you finish this challenge. Do not look at your computer until you finish this challenge.

After having your MBOs, exercise vigorously for as long as possible, with the goal being one hour. If you are used to exercising for more than an hour, then go longer. Whatever your level, challenge yourself to go as long and as hard as you can.

Do not turn your phone back on.

Treat yourself to a long shower or bath and put on an amazing costume that makes you look and feel like a star.

Do not turn your phone back on.

LEAVE YOUR PHONE AT HOME and treat yourself to lunch at a restaurant where you have never gone, or have

110

a picnic lunch in the park or by the river. Take something interesting to read, and actually read it.

After lunch, *do not* go home and get your phone.

Go experience a work of art without your phone. Go see a film, a play, or a concert, or visit a museum or art gallery.[1]

Throughout this challenge, repeat this mantra often: "I am Fearless, Independent, Relaxed, and Erotic. Everyone wants to sleep with me."

Make it your goal to speak to as many interesting strangers as possible and invite the most intriguing to your next dinner party.

Have No Expectations.

If participating online at NeverSleepAlone.com, write a brief and entertaining report detailing your experiences and impressions of the interesting strangers you met, and how it felt living without your mobile phone, and share it with me and the rest of the NSA Community.

---

[1] If you need directions to any of the places you want to go, write them down the night before so that you have no need to look at your phone or computer until the NSA Challenge is complete.

ATTENTION:

If you are still living your life with expectations and not having new experiences every day, if you are still going out with your friends all the time, and if you are not actively transforming your existence by adhering to the NSA Principle of STAR and consistently doing the 3 Things You Must Do on a regular basis, it is pointless to continue at this time.

Put the book down.

Turn your phone off.

Go exercise until you're exhausted and then masturbate until you have an MBO. Then light some candles, turn on some inspiring music, put on an amazing costume, and go someplace you have never been.

Alone.

Then you may continue.

NSA Principle 5

BDSM

Be Direct, Seem Mysterious

CAN YOU FEEL YOURSELF transforming into The One?

Do you realize that you are only just *beginning* to discover your limitless potential? Are you excited that you will soon have an all-access pass to the deep reservoir of socio-sexual power that lives within you?

I am so glad!

And if you start telling everyone you meet about NSA, and telling everyone all of the wonderful ways the NSA Program is changing your life, I *promise*, I will find you.

And I will kill you.

Because if you tell people about the work you are doing here, you will undo all of the work that has already been done.

It is time to get serious.

What you are about to learn will change your life.

If you can fully actualize this next NSA Principle, you

will not only be an Exceptional Individual, you will never feel empty inside again.

In order for you to truly understand how important this is, I want you to shout this out loud, right now:

"BDSM!"

Now I want you to read this silently, and don't say a fucking word.

Be
Direct
Seem
Mysterious

That is the key to happiness.

Be Direct, Seem Mysterious.

The more you say, the less people listen.

The less you say, the more people want to hear.

So, if you keep quiet, you are not giving people what they want.

And not giving people what they want is the fastest way to make people want YOU.

NSA TRUTH

People are most seduced by what
is most difficult to understand.

I *really* want to have sex with you.

I've been wanting to have sex with you for pages.

But, right now, if you were to tell me what you did this past weekend, I wouldn't want to have sex with you anymore.

And it's not because you aren't an amazing person. And

it's not because you didn't have amazing new experiences this past weekend.

It's because you don't know how to BDSM. You have no idea how to Be Direct and Seem Mysterious.

It's okay.

It's a *good* thing that you don't know how to do that yet. Almost *nobody knows how to do it.* And the few people who actually do know how to do it *can't make themselves do it.*

It's just like exercising.

And, just like exercising, if you know how to actualize BDSM, and you can actually make yourself do it often enough, you will become better than most people, which will make most people want to sleep with you.

What Is TRUE and What Is a LIE?

When someone asks you a question about yourself, your first instinct is to give a response that is TRUE:

When someone asks you about yourself, you tend to give a:

Tedious
Report (of)
Uninspiring
Events

The TRUE response is a direct betrayal of BDSM. It is not sexy and it is not interesting.

For the following example, let's say you are a woman. You meet a man at a bar and he asks you what you did this weekend.

If you were to ignore the rule of BDSM and give a TRUE response, the conversation would look something like this:

Him: So, what did you do this weekend?

You: Oh my god, sooooo much. My college roommate Jen decided to randomly come to town, so it was like, "Go go go!" On Friday night, I took her to this sick bar on Smith Street. We had wine and cheese and calamari. Actually, she had the calamari. I just ate the cheese plate because I'm a vegetarian. Then we went home and had a *Sex and the City* marathon 'cause that's, like, what we used to do back in the day. Then on Saturday, we went shopping for new fall clothes and I got this awesome bracelet totally on sale. Guess how much it was?

Him: Uh . . . I don't know, one hundred dollars?

You: *(shouting and hitting him in the shoulder)* No! Oh my god, it's, like, vintage Tom Ford, and it was supposed to be seven hundred fifty dollars but I got it on sale for three hundred dollars. I can't really afford it, but I just, like, wanted it so bad, you know? So I, like, got it as a present for myself. Anyways, we got all dressed up and looked amazing but still had to wait in line for, like, an hour outside of the club—

Him: *(looking at phone)* Sorry, my friend is texting me . . .

Disgusting.

There is a better way.

Learn to LIE

You are a star.

You have seen stars playing characters in movies and you have also seen stars "being themselves" in interviews.

During an interview, a star always knows what parts of their story to share and what parts not to mention. And a star always knows how to convey their story in a mysterious and intriguing way that makes people want to know more.

Because stars are not afraid to LIE:

Leverage
Interesting
Experiences

When you Leverage Interesting Experiences, you first decide which of your experiences are actually interesting. Then you make a conscious decision to heighten—or leverage—*only the most intriguing parts of that experience* when telling people about it.

Here is what the previous conversation looks like when you behave like a star and begin to actualize the principle of BDSM by remembering to LIE.

Him: What did you do this weekend?

You: Oh . . . *(smiles)* An old friend of mine came to town, unexpectedly.

Him: *(leaning forward)* Really? What did you guys do?

You: What *did* we do . . . ? *(leans back, takes a sip of wine, and looks off into the distance)* It's a bit of a blur. We did go dancing and we had some incredible meals, but mostly we just . . . enjoyed each other's company.

Him: Sounds like an amazing weekend . . .

You: *(smiles benevolently, says nothing, and lovingly adjusts bracelet)*

Him: Could I buy you another drink?

You: Yes. Thank you so much.

Him: That's a beautiful bracelet.

You: *(bittersweet sigh)* Thank you.

Him: *(leaning forward)* Where did you get it?

You: It was a gift.

Him: From who?

You: *(changing subject)* How was *your* weekend?

That's what it should look like.

You say, "But that's not who I really am!"

You are wrong.

You are so beautiful.

But you are so damn wrong.

And you need to be punished.

Put down the book.

And go spank yourself.

Ten times.

If you're ready to listen to me, you may turn the page.

If not, put down the book.

And spank yourself again.

It is very important to understand that BDSM is *not* about denying who you really are.

BDSM is about being confident enough in who you really are to sit back, relax, and *make the other person show you who they really are.*

You are a star.

You don't have to prove yourself to anyone.

In the first version of the above conversation, the woman forgot she was a star. She started talking way too much, revealing everything in an attempt to try to prove something to the person she was talking to. This made her seem desperate, it gave her *The Look of Expectation*, and it made the other person uncomfortable and sociosexually disinterested.

In the BDSM version, she sat back, relaxed, and remembered to LIE.

NSA TRUTH

LIEing is the fastest way to arrive at the truth.

It is important to note that everything she said in the BDSM/LIE version of the above conversation was 100 percent honest. She just Leveraged Interesting Experiences and revealed only the most intriguing parts of the story. She left out the tedious details and presented herself as a Fearless, Independent, Relaxed, and Erotic star of her own movie, which made the person she was talking to want to know more about her.

Also, because she stayed quiet, she began to learn a bit about the person she was talking to.

When talking to someone you find attractive, you must reveal only the most important and inspiring parts of your personal story and let the other person fill in the blanks with their imagination.

NSA TRUTH

A person will always be more turned on
by the things they imagine about you
than by the things you tell them about yourself.

Curiosity and desire.

BDSM is *not* about denying who you really are.

BDSM is *not* about intentionally deceiving others.

BDSM is about being a Giver.

And BDSM is about being a Receiver.

You are Giving the person you are talking to the gifts of mystery, excitement, and potential.

In return, you are Receiving the gifts of confidence, power, and peace.

Potential Energy vs. Released Energy

When you have just done something, or are thinking about doing something, you have Potential Energy inside you. The more you do and think about doing, the more that Potential Energy builds up inside you, giving you *The Aura of Experience*, that powerful and peaceful external glow we talked about when we discussed Principle 1, which is very intriguing and very attractive.

The more you do and think about doing, the more Potential Energy you create.

The more Potential Energy builds up inside you, the brighter your *Aura of Experience* becomes, and the more intriguing and attractive you become to whomever you are talking to.

But the moment you start telling someone about all the things you have done or are thinking of doing, you start releasing that energy. The more you talk and talk and talk, the more energy you release.

And once all the energy is released, it's gone forever.

NSA TRUTH

Every thing you do creates energy.
Every word you say destroys it.

If, when talking to a person, you talk too much and release all of your Potential Energy, you will feel empty inside. That emptiness will make you begin to *want* things from the person you are talking to. That wanting will give you *The Look of Expectation*, which, as we have discussed, is really fucking gross.

NSA TRUTH

Want nothing from no one
and everyone will want to give you everything.

Thus, if you release *all* of your Potential Energy too soon, you will feel empty, the person you are talking to will feel empty, you will look gross, the other person will feel gross, and nobody will have an MBO.

But if you actualize BDSM and keep that Potential Energy inside you, releasing only a tiny bit at a time, you will feel fulfilled and powerful. You will glow from within with *The Aura of Experience*. You will be Fearless, Independent, Relaxed, and Erotic.

The person you are talking to will feel very excited to be talking to you, and they will want to spend more time with you.

In order to Be Direct and Seem Mysterious, all you have to do is follow the 6 Rules of BDSM.

The first rule, you already know.

BDSM Rule #1: Always remember to LIE.

LIE =

Leverage
Interesting
Experiences

1. Think about the new experiences you've had recently.

2. Decide which of those new experiences are actually interesting.

3. Leverage Interesting Experiences by heightening and revealing only the most intriguing parts of the story, and don't mention the rest.

Easy.

Here are the other five rules of BDSM:

Rule #2: ADT

Rule #3: LT3

Rule #4: SSL

Rule #5: SMILE

And most important, **Rule #6: STFU**

Don't worry. I know it seems like a lot of rules. But they are all very easy to follow.

I will explain all of them and we will review with another sample BDSM conversation at the end of this section.

BDSM Rule #2:

ADT =

Ask
Don't
Tell

Whenever you have the urge to *tell* someone something about yourself, *ask* them something about themselves instead.

Easy.

BDSM Rule #3:

LT3 =

Less
Than
3

1. Whenever someone asks you something about yourself, limit your response to Less Than 3 sentences.

2. End every response by asking the other person another question about themselves.

Easy.

BDSM Rule #4:

SSL =

Stop
Saying
"Like"

You must eliminate the improper use of the word "like" from your speech patterns. It moderates feeling, interrupts passion, and makes smart and interesting people sound stupid and unfuckable. The misuse of the word "like" is one of the defining characteristics of the Mediocre Majority.

And you are an Exceptional Individual.

It is a very difficult thing to SSL, but once you can do it, you will be the most powerful person in every sociosexual situation.

You will find that if you do not allow yourself to say the word "like" when you talk, you won't be able to talk so damn much. The less you say the word "like," the less you will say. And the less you say, the more people want to hear . . .

It seems difficult, but it's actually easy.

1. Start watching yourself and other people.

2. Count how often you say "like" and how often other people say "like." You will notice that the sexiest and most confident people in the room are the ones who say "like" the least.

3. Stop Saying "Like" and watch how quickly you become the sexiest and most confident person in the room.

Easy.

Important: Do not tell people that you are trying to Stop Saying "Like." Doing so will make other people self-conscious and make you seem like an asshole. Once you have mastered SSL, you will become shocked and annoyed by how often everyone else says "like." Hold fast to your commitment to SSL, and lead by example. Eventually, people will emulate your good habits.

NSA TRUTH

Never stoop to conquer.
Inspire others to elevate themselves to your level.

BDSM Rule #5:

SMILE =

Smile

Smile.

Nobody smiles enough.

Smile.

Easy.

BDSM Rule #6:

This one is the most difficult.

But you are very capable of doing this.

STFU =

Shut

The

Fuck

Up

Most people do not have the ability to Shut The Fuck Up.

Most people find it impossible to stay quiet, maintain eye contact, SMILE, and listen to the other person during a one-on-one conversation. The very idea of these things scares the shit out of most people.

So, if you can fearlessly Shut The Fuck Up, SMILE, and make the other person talk while you actually listen, you will be a Fearless, Independent, Relaxed, and Erotic person and the people you talk to will find you very attractive and want to spend lots of time with you.

If you can keep quiet, maintain eye contact, and make the other person keep talking, they will begin to fear that *they* are mediocre and they will work harder and harder to please you.

1. When someone responds to a question you have asked, do not immediately comment on their response.

2. Do not immediately ask a follow-up question.

3. Sit back, SMILE, maintain eye contact, say nothing, and patiently wait for them to give you more.

4. Watch the other person become obsessed with you.

Easy.

———

That's it.

Those are the 6 Rules of BDSM.

It is important to note that in *most* cases, men need to work harder at Being Direct and women need to work harder on Seeming Mysterious.

Of the 6 Rules of BDSM, men need to work most on ADT and women need to work most on STFU.

The fastest way to get a woman to STFU is to buy her a drink and tell her she's beautiful.

The fastest way to get a man to buy you a drink and tell you you're beautiful is to STFU.

BDSM and You

Here is an example of a BDSM conversation between you and another person. You will see where the 6 Rules of BDSM come into play. We will call this other person Alex, since Alex can be either a male or a female.

Alex: Hi, I'm Alex. What's your name?

You: Hi, Alex. I'm _____ . What brings you here tonight? →**ADT**

Alex: I'm meeting up with some friends from work for some drinks and tapas, or like, whatever they're called. Not sure what we're gonna do later. What brings *you* here tonight?

You: I'm meeting someone for dinner later. →**LIE** I thought I'd →**SSL** have a drink first. →**LT3** Have you ever been here before? →**ADT**

Alex: Yeah, this is, like, one of my favorite bars. They have awesome cocktails.

You: They do. *(smiles)* →**SMILE**

Alex: Yeah, I come here, like, a lot because I work, like, right down the street at JPMorgan Chase. I work in investment banking.

You: *(Maintains eye contact. Smiles. Nods. Says nothing.)* →**STFU**

Alex: Yeah, I've been working there for, like, almost five years. I'm actually up for a big promotion. They tell me this week whether I got it or not.

You: *(Maintains eye contact. Smiles. Nods. Says nothing.)* →**STFU**

Alex: Yeah, I'm really excited about it because I'm, like, looking into buying a house soon . . .

You: *(Maintains eye contact. Smiles. Nods. Says nothing.)* →**STFU**

Alex: I want to get at least a three-bedroom. That way, if I, like, have kids one day . . . Do you want to have kids?

You: Hmm, I haven't really thought about it. →**LIE**

Stay Focused

When you BDSM, it is very important to remain 100 percent focused on the person you're talking to. You never look off into the distance or look around at other people. You smile, sit back, and maintain steady eye contact as though you are looking directly into their soul.

Sometimes, if the other person is very self-confident, they will focus more on you than on their own need to talk. They may try to get you to talk more and abandon your role as the BDSM dominant.

Here are the most common examples and ways you can counteract the situation:

If they say: "What are you thinking right now?"

You smile and say: "Nothing terribly important." (SMILE)

If they say: "Why are you being so quiet?"

You say: "Am I?" (ADT)

If they say: "I feel like I'm the only one talking."

You say: "I'm sorry. It's just so nice to talk to someone who actually has something interesting to say." (LIE)

The Power of BDSM

I know it seems strange.

In the beginning it will feel strange.

I know you are afraid to try it.

I promise it feels really good.

I know that the first time you try it, you will say: "It hurts."

I promise that though it hurts at first, after a while, it will make you feel better than you have ever felt in your entire life.

I promise that once you try it, you will get addicted to it. You will become so addicted to the rush of power that comes with BDSM that you will start doing it with everyone. You will try it not just on sexy strangers, but also on your friends, family members, and coworkers, and you will be shocked by the results.

NSA TRUTH

*It is only by learning to restrain yourself
that you will at last be free.*

If you can live your life according to the 6 Rules of BDSM,
you will become The One.

NSA CHALLENGE

Read and sign the BDSM contract on the following page.

This is a contract you are entering into with yourself, with me, and with the rest of the NSA Community, so you need to take it seriously. You need to understand what you are signing. Take it to a lawyer if you need to.

Once you sign the contract, you agree to live by the contract and uphold the 6 Rules of BDSM. Once you begin living by the NSA BDSM contract, you will live a more fulfilled life.

Sign the contract, scan it, and send it to me immediately through my e-mail: DoctorAlex@NeverSleepAlone.com.

I want a piece of you for always.

NSA BDSM *Contract*

I, _____, promise to uphold the NSA Principle of BDSM by making a conscious decision to always follow the 6 Rules of BDSM, outlined herein:

BDSM Rule 1: LIE = Leverage Interesting Experiences

I promise to Leverage Interesting Experiences by revealing only the most intriguing parts of my personal stories.

BDSM Rule 2: ADT = Ask Don't Tell

I promise that whenever I have the urge to *tell* someone something about myself, I will instead *ask* them something about themselves.

BDSM Rule 3: LT3 = Less Than 3

I promise that whenever someone asks me a question, I will limit my response to less than three sentences and end each response by asking that person another question.

BDSM Rule 4: SSL = Stop Saying "Like"

I promise to never misuse the word "like."
Ever.

BDSM Rule 5: SMILE = Smile

I promise to smile.
Always.

BDSM Rule 6: STFU = Shut The Fuck Up

I promise to Shut The Fuck Up.
For real.

Signed and agreed on this _____ day of _____ in the year _____

By:

_____

NSA Principle 6

PEEPs

Persons of Equivalent Erotic Potential

DO YOU HAVE ANY idea how lucky you are that you are not in a monogamous long-term relationship right now?

You may be thinking, "But I *want* one! Everyone I know who is in a monogamous long-term relationship is so happy all the time!"

They are lying.

Maybe they are happy some of the time. But the majority of their time is spent feeling annoyed, anxious, and/or horny. I guarantee you that more than 75 percent of the people who are constantly posting pictures of their partners and/or children on Facebook with status updates saying how blissfully happy they are really want to say, "Can I *please* just drink a goddamned cup of coffee *alone* this morning and go out and fuck a random stranger tonight?!"

When you are in a monogamous long-term relationship, you have to deny a part of yourself for the sake of the relationship. Because your needs and desires change moment by moment, there is no way that one other human being is capable of always giving you what you want, when you want it and how you want it.

Yet when you are in a monogamous long-term relationship, this other human being is *always around*, preventing you from pursuing your solitary pleasures, while not fulfilling all of your erotic needs. Therefore, when that other human being does not shower you with compliments, give you MBOs, and treat you like the sexual deity you know you are, you begin to resent them and yourself for missing out on all the great sex and MBOs you could be having with other PEEPs.

Right now, you are free.

You are free to get what you want, when you want and how you want, from whomever you want. You are free to have MBOs with many different people who can contribute many different things to your life while fulfilling your many erotic desires. You are free to learn more about yourself and sharpen your sexual skills while experiencing moments of euphoric happiness, exquisite pleasure, and real human connection. And you are free to do all of this without the expectations and obligations that come with a monogamous long-term relationship.

Once you have completed the NSA Program and become The One, everyone is going to want to be in a monogamous long-term relationship with you. If you enter into a relationship without the self-knowledge, sexual skills, and supreme confidence that come from having diverse sexual experiences, you are going to be incapable of pleasing your partner, your partner is going to be incapable of pleasing you, and your relationship is going to be doomed to failure.

Therefore, at this point in your NSA Journey, you are not allowed to seek a long-term relationship. Right now, your goal is to find as many PEEPs as possible to contribute to your immediate social and erotic pleasure and give you MBOs. Having diverse sociosexual interactions will help you build your confidence, sharpen your sociosexual skills, and learn more about who you really are.

Identifying and Accumulating PEEPs

When identifying Persons of Equivalent Erotic Potential, you need only concern yourself with the following criteria:

1. Do I want to sleep with this person?

2. Does this person want to sleep with me?

You don't have to worry about age, height, weight, income, occupation, immigration status, religious/political affiliations, life goals, or any other nonsense. All you have to worry about is whether you want to sleep with this person and whether this person wants to sleep with you.

We will talk more about Chemistry in the following pages, but remember, when you have sociosexual interactions with your PEEPs—whether it's a first conversation, a third date, or a monthlong fuckfest—you must never expect anything from them, other than immediate pleasure and mutual respect.

Because you are not concerned about having a future with your PEEPs, you can let go of your anxiety, be completely yourself, and live in the moment. You can feel perfectly comfortable asking for exactly what you want from them, in and out of bed, without fear of judgment or rejection. If someone isn't willing to give you what you want in and out of bed, wish them well and move on to the next PEEP as quickly as possible. Life is too short to not get what you want. But remember to treat every PEEP with utmost respect and make sure you get the same treatment in return.

People often ask me, "How do I find more PEEPs?"

You must make it a priority to always go to places where lots of single PEEPs hang out. You can find PEEPs at places such as sociosexual watering holes, singles events, enrichment classes, cultural and sporting events, fitness clubs, universities, airline lounges, hotel lobbies, and youth hostels. You must go to these places, and you must talk to absolutely everyone you find interesting and/or attractive.

There is no reason to fear beginning a conversation with someone. You now know how to BDSM; therefore, you will always be in control of every conversation you have. Also, you must remember, you're doing the other person a favor. Most people are shy and awkward and dying to talk to an interesting stranger, but they don't know how to begin a conversation.

You are a Fearless, Independent, Relaxed, and Erotic star who looks amazing, lives a beautiful and creative existence, loves everyone, and always has an interesting story to share. Do the other person a favor by being the one to initiate a conversation.

How To Initiate a Conversation

You can initiate a conversation with a PEEP by asking them an interesting question.

You can ask them a question about something they're wearing. You can ask them if they know of a good wine store in the area. You can ask them if they know an answer to a clue on your crossword puzzle. You can ask them if they know the bartender, because you find the bartender attractive. You can ask them anything you want.

Remember to BDSM throughout the conversation. If the conversation is going well and you feel you have Chemistry with this person, you should invite them to your next dinner party, or invite them to come with you to an event you are planning to attend in the near future.

Always invite PEEPs to specific parties or events, rather than just exchanging contact information. First invite them to a specific event and *then* exchange contact information, so that you can confirm a few days before the event is to take place.

Be Fearless

You must feel free to ask out[1] anyone you want and you must not fear rejection. If you have a fear of rejection, you

---

[1]A lot of heterosexual women say, "But a man is supposed to ask *me* out on a date!" You are not "asking a man out on a date." You are asking a sexually relevant human being to join you for a new experience. This is a new experience you are planning on having anyway, with or without the other human being. If you are a heterosexual woman, you should have no fear inviting men to your dinner party or to enjoy a new experience with you.

Dr. Alex Schiller

can't proceed with the book, because this means that you are not yet Fearless, and it means you are still living your life with expectations.

If you fear rejection, you must actively seek rejection by asking out as many people as possible who you believe will definitely reject you. You must get rejected over and over and over again until you realize that rejection is nothing to be afraid of and that it has nothing to do with you. It is Chemistry, and, as you will soon learn in the following pages, Chemistry is a force beyond your control.

You must also truly understand how rejection feels, because soon, *you* will be The One who is rejecting people, because your genitals will be tired and your schedule will be full. Therefore, you must actively seek rejection so you can learn the nicest way to deliver it to others.

You must fearlessly approach and ask out everyone you want. You must do so without expectations, and you must never make assumptions about whether someone is going to find you attractive, because you never know the circumstances surrounding the person you are approaching.

Perhaps they are extremely horny and they have decided they will sleep with the next person who asks them out. Perhaps they are nearly blind, and when they look at you, they see their favorite celebrity. Perhaps they have a fetish for your particular ethnicity, age, or body type.

Yes, if you are an overweight fifty-five-year-old man who hates his job, the bubbly eighteen-year-old art student with the full scholarship and perfect ass is *probably* not going to be attracted to you. But *maybe* she will be attracted to you. Maybe she wants to lose her virginity to someone who reminds her of her stepfather.

You never know.

So, GO.

I also recommend that you consider accepting invitations and dates from everyone, whether you find them sexually attractive or not, because doing so helps you actualize your NSA Principles while building your confidence and expanding your sociosexual network.

Expanding Your Sociosexual Network

You may not be attracted to Pat, the depressed tax accountant. But by saying yes and going to a party at Pat's house, you end up meeting Pat's friend Alex, who is a hot, happy painter. Because you said yes to depressed tax accountant Pat's invitation, you end up having amazing oral sex on Pat's bed with Alex, the hot, happy painter.

Inviting Kris, your mediocre neighbor, to join you for a drink at the new wine bar on your street puts you into contact with Izzi, the sexually dominant sommelier who asks for your phone number.[2]

Therefore, the fastest way to meet more PEEPs and expand your sociosexual network is by talking to everyone, asking out everyone, and accepting every invitation that fits into your schedule. Remember not to make your schedule so full that you don't have time to exercise, work on your creative

---

[2] Since your goal is to go out without your phone as often as possible, you must get a personal calling card made with your name, phone number, and e-mail address. Pick a paper that has a nice weight and sensual texture to it and create a design that is a reflection of who you are.

projects, and have new experiences alone, or you will end up extinguishing your FIRE. Make sure to keep at least two days and/or nights a week that are 100 percent yours.

Once you have expanded your sociosexual network, you must start having amazing sex and MBOs with everyone you want to have amazing sex and MBOs with.

The more sex you have, the more powerful you become. And the more sex you have, the better sex gets.

It's Now Or Never

One day, you will be old, weak, and sexually irrelevant and it will be too late for you. And then you will die with *The Look of Expectation* on your face, because you wasted the best years of your life being sexually repressed, when deep down, you wanted to be sexually liberated.

You have been brainwashed into believing that unless you are in a monogamous long-term relationship, you are nothing. And you have been brainwashed into believing that having lots of sex with lots of people is a bad thing, when exactly the opposite is true. If you use protection and make mutual pleasure and respect your goal, having lots of sex with lots of people is the best thing you can do for yourself, for your PEEPs, and for the rest of mankind.

I don't expect you to instantly abandon what you've thought you wanted all these years. Go ahead and keep perpetual monogamy as your ideal. But I want you to fully understand that your true value as a human being has *nothing* to do with your ability to secure a spouse, get married, and "live happily ever after."

It was never an inherent human desire to be perpetually monogamous. Your inherent human desire is to have as many MBOs as possible with as many PEEPs as possible. That is why when you have been in a monogamous relationship for an extended period of time and you and your partner have stopped having daily MBOs, you end up resenting each other and wanting to sleep with other people.

The idea that perpetual monogamy is the human ideal was invented and is perpetuated by churches, governments, corporations, and the aristocracy as a way to secure property, ensure paternity, and control the masses. The leaders of these institutions are almost never monogamous. They tell the uneducated and unenlightened masses that perpetual monogamy is the ideal so that the masses stay weak and easy to control. Because the more sex and MBOs you have, the more powerful you become.

You were put on this planet to have sex. That is your one true purpose in life. This is why, when you are having an MBO, you feel at one with the universe. You are fulfilling your destiny. You are doing what you were put on this planet to do.

Your brain may argue against this. Your brain may say, "I was put on this planet to make great art," or "I was put on this planet to make lots of money," or "I was put on this planet to be good to my friends and family." But your body is stronger than your brain. And your body wants sex. And if you don't give your body what it wants on a regular basis, it is not going to let your brain enjoy anything. No matter how impressive your nonsexual achievements are, your body is going to keep telling your brain, "You are not good enough."

The reason you feel so calm, beautiful, and powerful right after great sex is because your body has finally stopped fighting with your brain. After great sex, you will find that you think clearly, perform better at work, are kinder to your fellow humans, and finally see the world for the magical place it really is.

Therefore, the more PEEPs you meet, the more great sex you have, the more MBOs you give and receive, the more you will be able to actually enjoy the nonsexual moments of your life and have complete control over your existence.

NSA TRUTH

In order to think clearly,
you must fuck your brains out on a regular basis.

You are not some sexually irrelevant cog in the wheel of servitude that keeps the top tier of society sexually satisfied while you stay down in the mud with the rest of the Mediocre Majority as an insignificant slave, denying yourself pleasure and allowing your thoughts, feelings, and desires to be controlled by others.

Lay claim to your natural and inalienable right to give and receive MBOs whenever you want, however you want, and with whomever you want. Throw off your shackles and declare yourself the master of your sexual destiny.

Fuck the many.

Become The One.

NSA CHALLENGE

Secure two tickets to an interesting event you want to go to within the next two weeks. This can be a play, a concert, a sporting event, a wine tasting, a livestock auction—any event that you find personally interesting and exciting and that you will attend whether a PEEP accompanies you or not.

Do some research and find the places in your town where the most single PEEPs tend to hang out. Make it your goal to go to these places often and interact with as many PEEPs as possible, while projecting FIRE and actualizing BDSM.

Invite every PEEP you find interesting to attend this upcoming event with you, until one or more accepts. If more than one PEEP accepts, feel free to secure more tickets and take several PEEPs with you and/or invite these other PEEPs to one of your dinner parties.

Sleep with whomever you want, whenever you want.

Have No Expectations.

ATTENTION:

You really shouldn't need me to tell you this.

I don't care how old you are, where you are from, how many people you or your PEEP have or have not slept with; when you have sexual intercourse with someone, USE A FUCKING CONDOM!

You do not want to get a sexually transmitted infection or an unwanted baby! STIs and babies cost a lot of money and are often difficult and sometimes impossible to get rid of. So until you are ready and willing to deal with an STI or a baby, WEAR A CONDOM.

If someone tells you they are a virgin—CONDOM!

If someone tells you they love you—CONDOM!

If someone tells you they want to marry you—CONDOM!

If someone tells you they are on birth control—CONDOM!

If someone tells you they are sterile—CONDOM!

If someone tells you they were just tested for everything today and it all came back negative—CONDOM!

People LIE all the time.

Consider
Others'
Negligence
Desperation
Opinions (and)
Motives!

NSA Principle 7

C = FML

Chemistry = Fate Minus Logic

CHEMISTRY IS AN ASSHOLE.

Chemistry does not care about you, it does not care about me, and it does not care about your PEEPs.

You cannot predict Chemistry and you cannot control Chemistry.

You never know who you will have Chemistry with and who you will not have Chemistry with. You never know when Chemistry is coming and you never know when it will go away.

When Chemistry is there between you and a PEEP, you feel connected, fulfilled, and beautiful. When Chemistry is not there, you feel detached, depressed, and ugly.

Again, there is NOTHING you can do to control Chemistry.

It is stronger than you are.

But, the good news is:

You always KNOW when there is Chemistry.

AND

You always KNOW when there is NO Chemistry.

That is something you do not need me to teach you. You always know. You can feel it.

You will know within two minutes of meeting someone if they want to sleep with you and if you want to sleep with them.

If someone does not want to sleep with you, you must not take it personally.

It has *nothing* to do with you.

It's Chemistry.

And Chemistry is Fate Minus Logic.

Chemistry has *nothing* to do with how attractive you are, how interesting you are, or how well you are actualizing your NSA Principles. Chemistry is a force beyond your control.

FML.

Just as there is nothing you can say or do to convince

yourself to want someone who wants you when you do not want them, there is nothing you can say or do to convince a person who does not want you to want you. If someone does not want to sleep with you, you *must* get over it and move on to the next person as quickly as possible.

Because there is *nothing* you can do to change their mind. ***There is nothing you can say and nothing you can do to make someone who does not want you want you.***

NSA TRUTH

No amount of physics can alter Chemistry.

If you are talking to someone who *does* desire you, but you do not desire them, and there are no other sexually relevant people in the room, there is only one thing you can do.

Practice!

Practice actualizing your NSA Principles.

Practice opening up to this person, practice connecting with this person, practice seducing this person whom you have no Chemistry with so that you will both be more comfortable, confident, and relaxed when your real PEEPs show up. If we all use each other in that way, do you know what happens?

WAW.

We
All
Win

I talk to and sleep with people I'm not attracted to quite often. It's a great way to actualize NSA Principle 8 and it's a great way to build your sociosexual karma.

Also, because Chemistry comes and goes as it pleases, sometimes you will find yourself in the middle of a sociosexual encounter with someone you were totally unattracted to five minutes ago and—BAM!

All of a sudden Chemistry is there.

All of a sudden, someone is calling you "baby" and you fucking *love* it. All of a sudden, someone is giving you mouth-to-mouth champagne, and you feel at one with the universe. All of a sudden, you and that someone end up in the bathroom of a nightclub having MBOs. All of a sudden, you're slow-dancing in a fountain together at three a.m., making sweet and filthy love until the sun comes up, and passing out in each other's arms. All of a sudden you're waking up at noon, having MBOs until two, taking an hour-long shower together, having late brunch with their friends, and then going to the farmer's market to get things for dinner. All of a sudden, you're accepting a marriage proposal when you are at the height of your sociosexual power and have finally attained the ability to seduce whomever you want whenever you want.

FML.

In the same way Chemistry can come at any moment, it can leave at any moment. You can meet someone and have instant and undeniable Chemistry, stronger than anything either of you has ever known before. You can spend hours, days, months, years, decades with each other in complete sociosexual bliss.

And then one day, you wake up next to that person and think, "There is no longer any Chemistry here."

FML.

You know when the Chemistry is gone.

You must deal with it and you must get out of the situation as quickly as possible.

Because life is too short to be unhappy.

NSA TRUTH

Tomorrow your genitals could turn to dust.

I have known way too many people who stay in situations where there is no Chemistry, where there hasn't been Chemistry for a long while, and where deep down they *know* that Chemistry is not coming back. Yet they stay in that horrible situation, for hours, for days, months, years, decades, trying hopelessly to create Chemistry when it's impossible to do so; getting older and unhappier with every passing day; ignoring their desires; having no MBOs; turning into angry and depressed people; and then dying with *The Look of Expectation* on their face and decomposing into a pile of unfuckable dust.

Top Excuses for Not Leaving When the Chemistry Is Gone

1. *"I don't want to hurt the other person."*

You are already hurting them. Every time you are in the kitchen together, they feel like you are repeatedly stabbing them in the stomach with an electric knife. Every time you are in the bathroom together, they feel like you are dunking their head in the toilet and then squirting Listerine in their eyes. Every time you are in the bedroom together, they contemplate murdering you while you sleep.

2. *"I've invested so much in this relationship."*

Yes, and you got a lot out of your investment in the past. But this investment has stopped yielding returns. What *was* a good investment is now a bad investment and if you don't cut your losses now and get rid of that bad investment, it will poison the rest of your portfolio until you are emotionally and sexually bankrupt.

3. *"I don't want to be the one to 'lose.'"*

The game is over. The other player walked away a long time ago.

4. *"But we have so many great memories together!"*

Memories won't go down on you. And neither will the person you are with anymore. Go find someone who will.

The Good News

If you trust your instincts when they tell you there is no Chemistry and you have the courage to follow your instincts and get out of those situations as quickly as possible, Chemistry will always come back to you.

Because Chemistry always rewards smart and brave Exceptional Individuals who recognize their own worth and have the courage to leave unhappy situations.

If you flow with Chemistry and don't fight against it, you will always be happy. When Chemistry is there between you and a PEEP, accept it, appreciate it, and enjoy it. Don't say, "Oh, no! This is the *wrong* person to have Chemistry with." Or "This is not the right time to have Chemistry with someone!"

Just give in to the Chemistry and live fully in the moment. Enjoy every second of that easy and intense pleasure with whomever you are with, have some amazing new experiences together, and give and receive lots of Mind-Blowing Orgasms.

When Chemistry is not there, get the hell out of the situation.

As quickly as possible.

Do this, and Chemistry will always come back to you.

NSA TRUTH

First there is Chemistry.
Then there is no Chemistry. And then there is.

NSA CHALLENGE

If you live in a small town, drive (or take a bus, train, or boat) to the nearest major city where nobody knows you. If you live in a major city, go to either another major city near yours or the nearest small town with a large university.[1] *From this moment forward, you will be leaving your hometown at least once a month.*

Take a room for one or two nights at a local hostel or guesthouse. Hostels and guesthouses are always filled with single, attractive, and adventurous people from all over the world who are hungry for new experiences and MBOs. Thanks to globalization and the Internet allowing guests to review their experiences, hostels and guesthouses are now

---

[1] Even if you are over the age of forty, it is still a good idea to go to a university town and stay in a hostel or guesthouse. Universities, hostels, and guesthouses employ interesting and attractive people of all ages, many of whom are single, undersexed, overworked, and in desperate need of new experiences and MBOs.

some of the cleanest, most unique, and most affordable accommodations available. Imagine a boutique hotel with a common kitchen and bar that is always filled with single, attractive, and adventurous people who are hungry for new experiences and MBOs. I always stay at hostels and guesthouses when I travel alone. And I Never Sleep Alone.

Unless I want to.

You can find links to the best hostels and guesthouses at NeverSleepAlone.com.

Do research, talk to your hosts, and find the one bar or social event in this city or town where the *most* single PEEPs will be in attendance. Dress up in an amazing costume that makes you look like a sexy and intriguing journalist or psychology student. Go to the bar or event with a notebook and a pen.

Tell PEEPs that you are in town conducting a study on sociosexual chemistry and that you would like to interview them, because they seem interesting and attractive.

Tell them that all answers are confidential and that they will remain anonymous.

Interview ten PEEPs whom you find sexually attractive.

Interview ten PEEPs whom you find sexually unattractive.

Ask each PEEP the following questions:

1. Are you currently single? (If they say "No" without hesitation, thank them for their time and move on to the next person. If they say "Yes," "Sort of," "I'm not sure," "I just got out of something," or "No" with hesitation, proceed to question two.)

2. How soon after meeting someone do you know if you have Chemistry or not?

3. Have you had or would you ever have a sexual encounter with someone with whom you had no Chemistry?

4. You don't have to tell me which person, but have you ever had a sexual encounter with any of the people in this room?

5. You don't have to tell me which person, but do you want to have a sexual encounter with anyone in this room?

Notice when there is Chemistry between you and a PEEP and when there is not.

Learn to go with the flow of Chemistry without craving it or clinging to it.

If there is Chemistry between you and a PEEP, ask them additional questions. Remember that you are a Fearless, Independent, Relaxed, and Erotic star, and be sure to BDSM. Spend as much time with this PEEP as you'd like. If appropriate, exchange phone numbers, e-mail addresses, and/or MBOs.

If there is no Chemistry, move on to the next PEEP as quickly as possible.

Have sex with whomever you want, whenever you want.

Have No Expectations.

If participating online, write a detailed article about your evening and submit it to NeverSleepAlone.com to be considered for publication.

NSA Principle 8

PRO

Passionate, Reactive, Original

WHERE ARE YOU AND what are you doing?

You'd better not be sitting at home in sweatpants.

One day you will be forced to sit at home and wear sweatpants every day of your life, because you will be old, weak, and sexually irrelevant, and sweatpants will be the only thing that fits over your adult diaper.

So while you have a healthy and beautiful body and genitals that work properly, you should be out somewhere you've never been before, reading this book and radiating *The Aura of Experience*, while all the PEEPs in the room watch you out of the corners of their eyes and work up the courage to talk to you and give you Mind-Blowing Orgasms.

That's what you should be doing right now.

If you're at home right now, put the book down, make yourself look like a star, and go someplace new.

If you are already at a wonderful place looking like the Exceptional Individual you are, I will do my best to give you an MBO in your sleep tonight, and you may turn the page.

Has anyone ever offered you money for sex? If it hasn't happened to you yet, trust me, it will. Especially if you live in a small town.

Most people aren't used to seeing well-dressed, sexually satisfied people out alone, doing interesting things and being happy. So, if you are dressing like a star and actualizing all of your NSA Principles, some PEEPs may automatically assume you are a high-class prostitute.

This may happen to you whether you are a male or a female and you must never feel insulted. Take it as a compliment. Not only does this person think you are ready, willing, and able to have sex with whomever you want whenever you want—which, on its own, is a miraculous achievement that separates you from the Mediocre Majority and makes you an Exceptional Individual—but this person also believes, just from looking at you, that you are so sexy, so intriguing, and so skilled in the sociosexual arts that you can actually charge a lot of money for it!

That is the greatest compliment in the world.

You should never feel insulted if someone assumes you

are a prostitute, any more than you should feel insulted if someone assumes you are a computer programmer. Prostitutes and computer programmers both offer very specialized services that most people are incapable of or unwilling to provide to others in exchange for money. Prostitutes and computer programmers both speak specific languages that most people are afraid to learn, they both spend most of their adult lives working in dark rooms with poor ventilation, and they both perform tasks that, while seeming very difficult to outsiders, could actually be done equally well and at a much cheaper rate by a trained monkey.

But, there are two types of prostitutes and two kinds of computer programmers:

Type one is the *Mediocre Majority of Programmers and Prostitutes*. These people are workers, laborers, *slaves*. They are not very good at what they do, and deep down, they know that a monkey could do it better. They hate their jobs and they hate their customers. They always do only the bare minimum required to collect a modest fee, and they approach their work with a feeling of dread and disgust, because they feel trapped in their profession because it was the only skill they ever learned, they are too old or too lazy to switch careers, and/or they have kids to feed.

And then there is the Exceptional Elite of Programmers and Prostitutes. These people are pioneers, artists, *masters*. They are masters of themselves and they are masters of their art. They are masters of their own sexual destiny and the sexual destiny of others. They are amazing at what they do and they know that *nobody* could do it better. They love their work, they always exceed their clients' expectations, and they approach each assignment with a sense of happiness and gratitude, because they feel lucky that they are being paid well to do what they were born to do and that they can spend all of their working hours developing their craft and cultivating relationships without having to work at a restaurant to pay the rent.

These people are real pros. And people keep coming back to them time and time again.

And it's not because of *what* they do but *how* they do it.

A real pro knows that if you want to keep people

coming back for more, you have to do it the right way. You have to put your heart and soul into it.

You have to be:

Passionate
Reactive
Original

You must be Passionate by exhibiting an intense desire for your sexual partner. You must be Reactive by showing appreciation for the sexual pleasure you are receiving. And you must be Original by giving your partner a truly unique experience.

You must believe that you were put on this planet to give and receive sexual pleasure.

And *nobody does it better than you*.

If you listen to me, you will be the best sexual partner anyone has ever had, you will enjoy sex more than you ever have in your entire life, and PEEPs will want to keep coming back to you for more.

You Are Passionate

Most people are not Passionate.

Even if they have strong feelings, they are afraid to show them. Especially when they are having their first sexual encounter with a new partner. Most people believe that the first time they sleep with someone new, they are supposed to be cool and reserved.

They don't *want* to be like that, but they assume they *have* to be like that.

You are the opposite of those people.

You are not afraid to be Passionate because, as a pro, you know that deep down, your partner is yearning for a heightened experience that only *you* can provide. You provide this heightened experience by creating a cinematic environment for the seduction, by speaking with powerful language, by exhibiting an intense desire for your sexual partner, and by making your partner feel that their pleasure is your number-one priority in life.

As a pro, it is your duty to make each and every PEEP

feel like they are the most desirable person in the world.

A pro knows that the most effective way to do that is to LIE.

Ignore your PEEPs' shortcomings, focus on their desirable qualities, and then tell them how badly you want them.

But don't just say:

"Wow, you're so hot."

Or:

"I really wanna fuck you now."

That is the way mediocre prostitutes talk.

You are an exceptional pro who is the master of your sexual destiny and the sexual destiny of others. When you are having a sexual encounter with someone new, you must speak in a way that person has never been spoken to before. You must use poetic and passionate language and make them believe that you are *so* overwhelmed by your desire for them that all reason and logic have gone out the window.

You can say things like:

"Your perfect skin under my fingers is the proof I needed to believe in God."

Or:

"How is it that I've lived my whole life without smelling your hair?"

Or:

"I'm not a violent person, but I feel like I would murder someone right now, just to know what it feels like to be inside of you."

Or:

"I've never been spanked before, but something in your eyes tells me I deserve it."

Make sure that if you are a man, you say these things in a whispered tone into her right ear, with one hand firmly gripping the back of her neck and the other hand firmly gripping her ass.

Make sure that if you are a woman, you are in a position where you can say these things while looking up at the man with a mixture of fear, admiration, and animal lust.

Make sure that you and your PEEP have been kissing

for a long while before you use *The Language of Passion* or you will seem like a psycho.

Remember that most people are insecure about how others sensually perceive them. So if you really like a PEEP and you want them to feel comfortable in bed with you, passionately tell them how much you love the way they look, sound, smell, feel, and taste. Tell them you love the sound of their voice, the feel of their skin, the taste of their spit, and the tightness/hardness/softness/wetness of their whatever.

You can also compliment what they believe to be their most unattractive qualities—their long nose, their squeaky voice, their big ass, their small breasts, their pointy ears, their thick foreskin . . . tell them that you believe these to be very attractive qualities. Tell them you love the parts of themselves that they have always hated. This will put them at ease, make them feel extremely desirable, and allow them to truly enjoy the sexual encounter.

You Are Reactive

Most people are not comfortable enough to be Reactive the first time they sleep with someone new, because deep down, they fear that if they enjoy the experience too much, they will give their sexual partner too much power.

Most people lie there like a dead fish.

You are the opposite of those people. You are not afraid to openly express your appreciation for the sexual pleasure you are receiving because, as a master and as a pro, you know that being very Reactive is the way to ensure that *you have all the power*.

I'm going to tell you a very big secret now.

The key to having ultimate sexual power over another person is to **make that person believe that they are the best lover you have ever had.**

Ever.

That is how you keep them coming back for more.

Because everyone wants to be The Best at something.

And nobody ever is.

Most people do not have the confidence, the skill, or the stamina to be The Best at anything. They have tried to be The Best several times throughout their life, and they have always failed. Unless you are sleeping with an Olympic gold medalist, a Grammy/Oscar/Tony winner, or the president of a major country, you are most likely sleeping with someone who has never been The Best at anything in their adult life.

And that's the one thing they have always wanted.

So, if you can make them believe that they are The Best lover you have ever had, they will have a sense of power and peace that they have never felt before. They will become addicted to this feeling, which will make them become addicted to YOU, and they will keep coming back to give you MBOs time and time again, because having sex with you is the one area in their adult life in which they have actually succeeded.

So, make sure that every time a new partner gives you an MBO, you lie back with a look of amazement and say, in an awestruck and grateful tone, "You just gave me the most intense orgasm of my life."

You Are Original

Most people are boring and unimaginative lovers the first time they have sex with a new partner. They believe that if they try something unique or exciting, their partner will "freak out" on them and think they are "weird."

You are the opposite of those people. When you have a sociosexual encounter with someone, they feel that everything you do, in and out of bed, is refreshing and unusual.

Most PEEPs will be completely impressed by your originality before you even get them into bed. If you have been actualizing all of your NSA Principles and have No Expectations for the experience, and they didn't have to deal with your annoying BFF, and you managed to STFU for more than two minutes, and you two actually have Chemistry, this is already the most Original sociosexual encounter they have ever had in their life.

But, if you want to be even more Original, and you feel your PEEP is adventurous enough, you can take it to the next level by trying one of the more unique moves in your Sexual Repertoire.

Your Sexual Repertoire is the stock of impressive sexual acts that you are very comfortable performing. Your Sexual Repertoire should contain classics such as Blow Job, Finger Banging, Doggy Style, and Roman Cupcake, but it should also contain a few acts that are more edgy and unique.

I have built up my Sexual Repertoire over the years by having lots of new sexual experiences with diverse peoples, watching pornography from every decade and every culture, attending sex parties, and observing others.

You must do the same.

You must know what PEEPs like to do in bed and you must know what you like to do in bed. And you must practice often.

You can also go to a bar where there are a lot of drunk and horny people, pretend to be a journalist from a popular publication, and ask people what was the best and most unique sex move someone ever tried on them. You can then put *their* favorite acts into *your* Sexual Repertoire and claim them as your own.

You can also hire a prostitute.

You are welcome to try out any of the acts from my Sexual Repertoire and claim them as your own. Below are three of my personal favorites.

These acts will all work equally well on males or females.

1. The Kissing Orgasm

I learned this from a very nice boy from Naples, Italy, after he reupholstered the interior of my car.

Lie next to your partner in bed and say, in a soft, deep, and confident tone, "I bet I could give you an orgasm just by kissing you. But you have to keep your eyes closed and you have to stay completely still. You can't move at all."

Once they agree, begin to kiss them very lightly, first on their neck, and then plant soft kisses across their jawline, on their cheeks and eyelids, and finally on their lips. Kiss their lips softly and teasingly for a minute or two, and then begin to lick their lips very gently. After a minute, increase the pressure slightly, as though you are trying to part their lips with your tongue. Continue this for another minute and then begin to French kiss them, softly at first, and then more passionately. Explore every part of their mouth with your tongue and lips.

Take your time.

Imagine that you are making love to this person's mouth in a sensual, confident, slow, and masterful way. Imagine that your tongues are becoming one. Tune in to the Chemistry between the two of you and develop your own rhythm.

If it helps, you can imagine that you two are both young teenagers at a sleepaway summer camp in New England and that this is your first sexual experience, or that you are Romeo and Juliet under a canopy bed in fair Verona, or Tristan and Isolde on the mossy floor of the forest of Morrois, or mean jock stepbrother and shy bookish stepsister in the aboveground swimming pool at a trailer park in Mait-land, Florida.

Whatever you are imagining, do not tell the other person in words. Tell them wordlessly, with your tongue and with your mind. They will begin to squirm about in intense ecstasy. If they try to move, hold them down gently with one hand and say softly, "Behave yourself. You promised not to move."

After about five minutes, if they have not had an MBO yet, you can use your hand on their genitals in a slow, firm yet gentle, consistent manner, and/or guide their hand to their own genitals. Keep kissing them passionately and patiently, as though you never intend to stop until the day they die.

They will climax within sixty seconds.

2. *Spontaneous Role Play*

While you are engaged in a sociosexual encounter, instantly and without provocation or discussion, assume the role of a sexy and unique character and continue with the sexual encounter as though you are this new person. If you act with utmost confidence and create intriguing scenarios, using sexy dialogue without laughing or breaking character, your partner will automatically assume a complementary role and you two will have Mind-Blowing Orgasms.

Here are some examples of characters and opening dialogue:

VIP Service: This is my personal favorite.

I have done this several times to many different PEEPs, including my American husband, my Croatian lover, my French ballet teacher, and a Backstreet Boy.

When you and your partner arrive at your home, kiss them at the door and ask them to wait outside a moment. Quickly dim the lights, light a few candles, turn on lounge music, and, if appropriate, take off your shirt. If you have a wig, dark vest, or geisha robe available, put it on, quickly. Then open the door a bit and peek out as though you don't recognize your partner. Look at them blankly and say in a flat, low tone, "Can I help you?" or "What's the password?"

Then "recognize" them and say apologetically, "Oh,

I'm so sorry, Mr./Miss/Ms./Mrs. [insert your partner's last name]. We haven't seen you in so long! Do come in. I'm dying to hear what sort of adventures you have been up to. What will you be drinking tonight?"

They should get the hint and assume the role of a rich VIP who has a sexual desire for you. Bring them their drink and then say, obsequiously, "Would you like me to sit and drink with you like last time, sir/miss?" Put your hand on their leg, tentatively, and then continue the conversation in a flirty yet professionally detached manner.

When they try to get physical with you, let them for a moment, as though your desire for them has gotten the better of you. Then break off suddenly, look deeply into their eyes, and whisper, "Forgive me, my darling," and ask them for their credit card.

The Teacher: Ask your PEEP to do something simple yet sensual, such as lighting candles, getting something off a high shelf, or giving you a shoulder rub. After they have completed the task say, "Thank you very much, [insert your partner's first name]. That was very good. I should make you stay after class more often. Did you finish your essay?"

The Student: As you are entering your partner or your partner is about to enter you, say, "Shhh. We have to be quiet. I don't want my dad to hear."

3. Spontaneous Anal Play

Self-explanatory.

Important

Keep in mind that unless your PEEP is very adventurous and open-minded you should probably wait until the second or third time you sleep together to try out the more advanced acts in your/my Sexual Repertoire. The truly important thing to remember during your first sexual encounter with a new PEEP is that you must make them believe that *they* have done something Original for *you*.

Because if you can make your PEEP believe that

something they did to you or with you was "a first" for you, they will feel incredibly sexy and very powerful, as though they have discovered some secret and sensual part of you that nobody else has ever seen before. They will feel a rush of triumph, creation, and discovery, as though they were a Roman gladiator, a Greek goddess, or Christopher Columbus.

They will become addicted to this feeling, which will make them become addicted to *you*.

Because everyone wants to be The First at something.

And nobody ever is.

So, the first time you sleep with a new PEEP, be sure to make them believe they are The First at doing something to you or with you. You can tell them they're the first to give you multiple orgasms. Or that they are the first foreigner you have ever slept with. You can say that this was the first time you begged to be tied to a kitchen chair and spanked with a flip-flop.

It really doesn't matter what it is, or if you actually *have* done it before. Just do something somewhat interesting with your PEEP, and after the sexual experience is over say, "Wow, I've never done *that* with anyone before."

And kiss them in a Passionate, Reactive, and Original way.

They will keep coming back for more.

Cultivate Erotic Dependencies

A pro knows that a surefire way to keep PEEPs coming back for more is to identify a person's deepest, darkest erotic desires and fantasies, and fulfill them. Nearly every human being on earth is dying to try some freaky shit in bed, but they are afraid to ask for it. So, if you can find out what your PEEPs' secret sexual desires are and fulfill them, they will keep coming back to you time and time again and they will become a slave to *your* desires, because you are the only person who is capable of fulfilling theirs.

The best way to get someone to reveal their secret sexual desires is to reveal one of yours. It is best to do this during sex, during foreplay, or when you're having a sexually charged conversation. Say to the person, "Can I tell you a secret? I've never _____ before and I've always wanted to. Do you think that's strange?"

As long as it's not illegal, they will not think it's strange. If they *do* think it's strange, you don't want to sleep with them again anyway. If you avoid fantasies about animals, minors, cadavers, and members of your immediate family, I guarantee your PEEP will be extremely turned on that you shared your secret desires, and they will want to fulfill your fantasy.

After they fulfill your fantasy, you can tell them you want to thank them by fulfilling one of theirs. They will reveal their fantasy, you will fulfill it, and you two will have crazy, filthy, beautiful sex and MBOs with each other however you want and whenever you want.

The Importance of Communication

A pro knows everybody is different and that every *body* is different. Just as you have certain things you like and certain things you hate in bed, every person you sleep with is going to have different sexual preferences. What makes one penis ejaculate might make another penis go limp. What makes one woman have multiple orgasms might make another woman slap you across the face.

Most PEEPs are going to be too nervous the first time you sleep together to tell you what they want and how they want it, and they are going to be too nervous to ask you what you want and how you want it. So, as the pro in the situation and the master of your sexual destinies, it is your job to make sure you are both communicating with each other throughout the sexual experience and you are both getting what you want.

You can say things like, "You're soooo good. Am I doing it the way *you* like it?"

Or, "I want to make you feel as good as you make me feel. Tell me how you like it."

Remember that *your* pleasure is just as important as your PEEP's pleasure. So always be very clear with your partner about what you want and how you want it.

But like a pro, you must always offer constructive criticism in a sexy and positive way. If a PEEP is not doing it the way you like it and you want them to change their technique, don't say, "Ow! Fuck! You're doing it wrong, damn it!"

Like a pro, begin every constructive criticism with a kind compliment. Kiss them and say, "You're sooo sexy. Now can we try it a little slower [or faster, or harder, or softer]? Yessss. You are so good. Keep doing exactly that, please."

NSA TRUTH

Give a man a fuck, and he'll come once.
Teach a man to fuck,
AND HE'LL KNOW HOW TO FUCK.

And if they are doing it exactly the way you like it, be sure to tell them often. And always be very personal in your praise.

Never say:

"*That* is so good."

Or:

"*That* is so perfect."

Always say:

"*You* are so good."

Or:

"*You* are so perfect."

A pro knows that people want to be treated like children. But not ugly, stupid, unwanted children. People want to be treated like pretty, gifted, and spoiled children. That's why grown women are obsessed with cupcakes and grown men are obsessed with breasts.

So, remember to always make your sexual partner feel like they are doing a *good job*!

Also remember, the whole point of sex is that it is supposed to feel amazing for all parties involved. The only way for this to happen is if all parties are communicating often. As the pro, during the sexual encounter you must never be afraid to ORGASM.

Dr. Alex Schiller

Offer
Regular
Guidance
And
Sometimes
Money

I'm not saying you should pay for sex. After all, you are the pro here. But from experience, I can tell you that offering someone money while at the height of passion is one of the sexiest things you could ever do.

One time, during Fleet Week, a young sailor from Israel was going down on me. Since most young Israeli men seldom go down on women, he was very bad, at first. But, after I'd given him some kind compliments and constructive criticism, he finally got into an amazing rhythm and I knew if he just kept going at exactly that speed for two more minutes, I would have an MBO. But I also knew that since he'd already been at it for more than fifteen minutes, he was probably getting tired and might quit at any moment.

So, I pressed myself against his tongue, wrapped my legs around his neck, and moaned, "God, I will give you a thousand dollars if you just keep doing exactly that."

He kept going.

I kept coming.

WAW.

NSA TRUTH

If you treat them like a pro, they will do it like a pro.

He didn't ask for the money.

But he certainly earned it.

The Importance of Oral Sex

You must be willing and able to provide transcendentally good oral sex to your sexual partners. Oral sex is great for you, it's great for your partner, it's great for your skin, and it won't make you pregnant.

Women, I don't want to hear:

"I have a sensitive gag reflex."

Or:

"I don't like putting things in my mouth."

You've got no problem putting that giant designer cupcake in your mouth and *swallowing* all that buttercream icing.

And, men, I don't want to hear:

"I can only do it if I really like her."

Or:

"What if she's not clean?"

She's clean, bro. The vagina is a self-cleansing ecosystem.

GDGH.

Dr. Alex Schiller

GO DOWN.

Or GO HOME.

Almost nobody wants a sex partner who does not like oral sex. You need to do it. You need to do it extremely well. And you need to keep doing it until your partner tells you to stop.

I want you to look at giving oral sex like running a marathon. If you train hard, maintain a consistent pace, and finish strong people, will think you're a god, and you will get lots of free stuff.

If you are nervous that you don't know what to do during oral sex, watch porno videos, attend classes, or hire a prostitute to teach you some things, and then be sure to practice, practice, practice on lots of people, until you feel like a master of this very important art.

Honestly, because every PEEP is different, technique can take you only so far. It's really all about Chemistry and psychological manipulation. Chemistry is easy to detect and people are easy to manipulate, so just actualize your NSA Principles while being Passionate, Reactive, and Original, and the technique will come naturally.

You Have All the Time in the World

A pro knows that it is important to take time and truly savor every moment of the sexual experience. A pro also knows that the best way to help someone have an orgasm is to assure the other person that you have all the time in the world. Because when someone is taking forever to have an orgasm, it's usually because they are anxious that *you* are annoyed that they haven't had an orgasm yet. And that anxiety keeps them from having an orgasm.

So, if you are starting to get bored, tired, or annoyed that the other person is not having an orgasm, just behave as though you are excited, energized, and in complete ecstasy. Continue pleasuring them with your hand, mouth, or genitals, and say one or both of the following:

"God, you look/feel/taste so amazing. I could do this all night long."

Or:

"Be careful, sexy. If you come it's going to make me come."

They will orgasm within two minutes.

Dr. Alex Schiller

$\bigvee$

NSA CHALLENGE

The next time you have sex with someone, imagine that you are the highest-paid prostitute who ever lived. Imagine that you are known worldwide for your social charms, sensual aesthetics, and sexual prowess. Imagine that your sexual partner is the richest person in the world and that they have been on a waiting list for six months, just to spend one night with you.

Throughout the entire experience, remember to be Passionate, Reactive, and Original. If they are doing an amazing job, make sure to say repeatedly, "You are so perfect. You are The Best."

Once you have both received enough MBOs, make a noise of contentment and exhaustion and collapse next to your PEEP. Look around, shocked, dazed, confused, and extremely satisfied. Then say:

"That was the most intense orgasm of my life."

Enjoy the post-MBO glow for ten minutes or less. Then take the following appropriate action depending on the location and situation:

A) If you are at their house and you sense they want you to leave, get dressed quickly and leave.

B) If you are at their house and you sense they want you to stay, get dressed quickly and leave.

You are a star and you are a pro.
You have things to do and places to go.

C) If they are at your house and you want them to leave, kiss them deeply and say: "Thank you for this. I feel so *inspired* now. I have so much work to do, but can I get you anything or do anything for you before you go home? You're so amazing." Then turn on your computer, look at your cell phone, and start scribbling down important things in your notebook.

D) If they are at your house and you want them to
stay, say, "If you'd like to stay, please do. Relax
and enjoy yourself and I'll be back very soon.
I need a few minutes to sketch out some ideas
for a project I'm working on. Would you like
a hot shower or bath?" Leave them a freshly
laundered rolled-up towel, show them where
your clean bathroom is, kiss them tenderly,
and go work on one of your creations for a half
hour. Then come back into the room, offer
them a hot tea, a glass of wine, some freshly
chopped pineapple, and/or another MBO.

Repeat with 1–30 other PEEPs this month.

NSA Principle 9

RIP

Remain In Power

IF YOU WANT TO Never Sleep Alone, after an amazing sociosexual encounter, you must:

Remain
In
Power

When you Remain In Power, you do not delude yourself into thinking anything you say or do will allow you to control someone else. When you Remain In Power, you maintain control over *yourself*.

After an amazing sociosexual encounter, you must maintain control over your emotions, you must maintain control over your thoughts, and most important, you must maintain control over your actions.

Most people can't do that.

Most people lose complete control over their emotions, thoughts, and actions after an amazing sociosexual encounter. They neglect their personal needs and desires, abandon their independent existence, waste all their time and energy obsessing over another human being, and backslide into the mud with the rest of the Mediocre Majority.

You are better than those people.

You are a Fearless, Independent, Relaxed, and Erotic star who is quite capable of controlling your emotions, thoughts, and actions. After an amazing sociosexual encounter, you don't cling to the experience, and you don't cling to the other person—

You get the hell out of bed and get back to doing the things that are important to *you*.

NSA TRUTH

In order to be missed, you have to leave.

You do not waste your precious time on this planet analyzing everything the other person says and does, manipulating your schedule and adjusting your desires to fit around the other person's, or having expectations for your future together. You spend that time having new independent experiences, working on your creative projects, and improving your body and mind.

You are not afraid to be alone and you are not dependent on the actions or approval of another human being. You keep your individual needs and wants as your top priority, and you desire yourself above all others.

NSA TRUTH

Desire yourself and
you shall always be desired.

There are a lot of people in this world. A lot of people who want to give you love and sex and MBOs. You must remember that. As long as you hold true to yourself and Remain In Power, you will become The One who everyone wants to be with.

The second you stop caring about creating an independent life of beauty, creativity, and passion, the second you begin to rely on someone else for your happiness, that is the second you start losing your power and regressing back to being just another member of the Mediocre Majority whom nobody wants to sleep with.

You are not going to regress.

You are going to Remain In Power for the rest of your life.

You are going to allow yourself to fall in love with whomever you want, whenever you want, for as long as you want. But you are never going to allow your feelings for another human being to make you abandon your individual existence and cease being the Exceptional Individual you worked so hard to become.

It is very difficult to Remain In Power when you enter into a romantic relationship because human beings enable each other to regress toward mediocrity. This is why many couples get fat, start wearing sweatpants every night, stop having new experiences and MBOs with each other, and eventually start wanting to sleep with other people.

People do not want to be with people who enable them to be mediocre. People want to be with people who inspire them to become Exceptional. It is difficult at times, but you must Remain In Power, lead by example, and inspire your romantic and sexual partners to elevate themselves to your level.

Even if you get married and have children, you must still Remain In Power. You must still seek out new experiences every day of your life. You must still go out alone and travel often, wear beautiful costumes every day, and live in an exquisite environment. You must still have dinner parties every two weeks, dedicate time for daily creation, and arouse the curiosity and desire of everyone you meet.

You must continue to strive to have MBOs, exercise,

and live without your phone as often as possible. You must stay Fearless, Independent, Relaxed, and Erotic. You must Be Direct and Seem Mysterious, flirt with PEEPs, go with the flow of Chemistry, and always be a Passionate, Reactive, and Original lover.

Because that is who you are.

Stay Exceptional.

Become The One.

NSA CHALLENGE

Turn off your cell phone, go to a quiet place alone, and spend one hour examining your life and answering the following questions.

If you can honestly answer yes to all of the questions, you will complete your transformation into The One.

If you can't, you won't.

NSA Principle 1

NSA = NSA

Am I actualizing the principle of Never Sleep Alone = No Strings Attached by actively seeking new experiences and having No Expectations for any experience?

NSA Principle 2

BFF = UCB

*Am I actualizing the principle of Best Friend Forever =
Ultimate Cock Block by going out alone and experimenting
with different personas and sociosexual roles, while actively
planning a solo vacation to an international location?*

NSA Principle 3

STAR

*Am I actualizing the principle of Style Transcends Actual
Reality by constantly creating a beautiful and cinematic
existence, arousing the curiosity and desire or everyone I
meet, and living as the seductive, adventurous, and inspiring star of my own movie?*

NSA Principle 4

FIRE

*Am I actualizing the principle of FIRE by being a Fear-
less, Independent, Relaxed and Erotic person by having*

MBOs often, exercising regularly, and living without my mobile phone as often as possible?

NSA Principle 5

BDSM

Am I actualizing the principle of Be Direct, Seem Mysterious by being an intriguing and generous conversationalist who is confident enough to sit back, SMILE, listen, and let the other person reveal themselves to me?

NSA Principle 6

PEEPs

Am I expanding my sociosexual network of Persons of Equivalent Erotic Potential by actively seeking out multiple people to contribute to my immediate pleasure and sociosexual growth, rather than desperately searching for one specific person to fulfill all of my needs and desires?

NSA Principle 7

C = FML

Am I actualizing the principle of Chemistry = Fate Minus Logic by accepting Chemistry as an ever-changing force (asshole) and not taking it personally when there is no Chemistry between another human being and myself?

NSA Principle 8

PRO

Am I a Passionate, Reactive, and Original Master of Sexual Destinies who always strives to give every sexual partner a unique and pleasurable sexual experience while openly communicating my sexual needs and desires?

NSA Principle 9

RIP

Am I actualizing the principle of Remain In Power by maintaining control over my emotions, thoughts, and actions;

not allowing myself to regress to mediocrity; and loving and desiring myself above all others?

You must revisit this list every week and you must remember that NSA is a lifelong journey. If there is a week where you can't honestly answer yes to all of these questions, you must revisit your 9 NSA Principles, repeat the NSA Challenges as often as necessary, and strive to improve in those areas where you are lacking. What separates you from the Mediocre Majority is your consistent desire to lead the beautiful and inspired life of an Exceptional Individual.

The One does not give up when things get difficult.

The One keeps going.

Congratulations

By completing the NSA Program, you have done what most people are incapable of doing. You have faced your fears, you have overcome your inhibitions, and you have worked your ass off to transform your existence and become the Exceptional Individual you were always meant to be.

I am so proud of you.

Most people will *never* do what you have done.

Most people will waste their lives being fearful and mediocre, and die with *The Look of Expectation* on their sad and sexually irrelevant faces.

But *you*, my beautiful and powerful Exceptional Individual, are going to live the enchanted and enviable life that others only dream about. You are going to have new experiences, you are going to visit exotic places, you are going to meet beautiful people, and these people are going to want to sleep with you.

From this moment forward, you will Never Sleep Alone.

Unless you want to . . .

Dr. Alex Schiller

You're The One.

A Note from Dr. Alex

IF YOU ARE NOW living every day of your life fully actualizing the 9 NSA Principles, you are now capable of having
the sociosexual life you always wanted.

You must now answer the following question:

What kind of sociosexual life do I want?

You must ask yourself this question every day. And
you must embrace the fact that your answer may change.
Today, you may want to have random sex with a complete
stranger; tomorrow, you may want to enter into a monogamous long-term relationship; the day after tomorrow, you
may want to get gangbanged; the day after that, you may
want to be a born-again virgin; and the day after that, you
may want to be a homosexual.

And that is okay. You are a human being. You have

needs, you have desires, and you should never be afraid to fulfill them.

You get only ONE LIFE, and you should live every precious moment exactly as you want.

Never forget that every sexual encounter is an opportunity for self-discovery, euphoric pleasure, and true human connection. Whether your sexual partner is a random stranger, your spouse of twenty years, or your drunk fraternity brother, you must always aspire to have the best sexual experience of both your lives.

Never forget that you are beautiful, never forget that your partner is beautiful, and never forget that sex is beautiful. And never forget that every time you have sex . . . it could be the last time.

Tomorrow your genitals could turn to dust.

But right now, in this moment, you are younger and sexier than you will ever be again.

So, go have some new experiences.

Go be the star of your own movie.

Go give and receive MBOs all over this beautiful, magical world.

Go get whatever you want, whenever you want, and however you want, with whomever you want.

Because you deserve it.

You're The One.

Love,

Dr. Alex

Get email updates on

ALEX SCHILLER,

exclusive offers,

and other great book recommendations

from Simon & Schuster.

Visit **newsletters.simonandschuster.com**

or

scan below to sign up:

*To my wife, your smile warms my heart,
your laughter lifts my spirit, and your love
refreshes my soul.*

*To my husband, my friend and consistent prayer warrior,
you have listened to my dreams and helped to make them
come true. Your relentless and unconditional love
continuously breathes life into me.*

Other Books

Dr. T. Cedric Brown

Ministry of the Towel
Serving God by Serving Others

Bobette Brown

Jesus Said, "Come"
Trusting God as You Walk by Faith

Be a Water Walker
You Can Defy the Odds

Ladies in Waiting
31-Day Devotional for All the Single Ladies

Daily Dose of Direction for Women in Business
*A 90-Day Journey to Direct and Guide Women in
Business to Succeed*
(co-authored with Melanie Bonita)

The Legacy Project: Empowering the Next
Generation of Ministry Leaders
A Compilation of Essays
(co-authored with Melva McGlen)

Contents

Introduction

Marriage is a divine institution ordained by God. In other words, marriage is God's idea. He created it and designed it. Many people have attempted to create their own version of marriage, but God is the originator. There is no substitute or equivalent for this holy union. Marriage works best when done the way that He intended it to work.

Dr. Myles Monroe, former pastor and founder of the Bahamas Faith Ministries International, once said, *"If you want to know the purpose of a thing, you must ask the Creator of the thing, not the thing."* Why do we ask so many different people the purpose of marriage, or seek out countless resources on how to establish a successful marriage instead of simply asking *the Author* of marriage itself – our God, the Father?

In society, we often rely on media personalities and popular public figures to guide us in properly performing our roles within the marital relationship. Some of us have even duplicated the unhealthy models of marriage that we witnessed growing up.

As ministers, we have both seen unhealthy examples of marriage and have also witnessed marriages that perform according to God's standard. We don't believe that men and women enter marriage with the expectation of becoming a bad example.

People sincerely desire to do it right! Unfortunately, for too many, they have developed their own way of doing marriage instead of following God's plan and purpose for marriage.

In this book, we present not a new model of marriage, but the *biblical* model of marriage. By drawing from our own personal experiences and discussing many of the lessons that we have learned along our shared journey, we seek to shine a light on marriage from God's perspective. We firmly believe that any other perspective is false and will not yield the results that we all truly desire.

As of the writing of this book, we are nearly 30 years into our marriage relationship, and our marital story is still being written today. We understand more than ever, that "iron sharpens iron" and we have certainly endured our own seasons of pain, misunderstanding and friction. But we are committed to stand firm, rooted and grounded in God's Word. As a couple, we hold fast to the enduring biblical truth that "we can do all things through Christ who gives us strength."

We do not claim to know it all. As you will discover in the pages of this book, we still have our share of ups and downs, even to this day. But we are committed to openly and honestly sharing what we have learned through our marriage in the hope that it will empower and inspire you.

We have worked together on the writing of this book. As you will see, throughout chapters 1 to 3 we have chosen to lend our voices separately. Nevertheless, as a couple, our values and beliefs in the institution of marriage are united by the Word of God and our love for Jesus Christ.

It is our sincere prayer that as you read the pages of this book, you will listen to the Holy Spirit's guidance beyond the many words and stories contained in these pages. You will certainly laugh, and you may even cry. But do take time to reflect. Take notes on the pages. Share your discoveries with your spouse or friends. Remember, where there is unity, there is also strength.

1

Unity in Diversity

"Strength lies in differences, not in similarities."

~ Stephen Covey

I should have seen it coming a mile away. We had just completed a busy season of business meetings across the country, counseling sessions with dating and married couples, and ministry-related events across our various partner churches. I was exhausted.

As we walked up to the front desk of a beautiful beach-front hotel in Cancun, Mexico for a much-needed week of vacation, I breathed an internal sigh of relief.

This was finally our opportunity to relax and unwind – no schedules to review, no phone calls to return, no text messages to read, no counseling session to administer, just blissful peace and tranquility under the glorious Mexico sun. For a moment, my eyes glazed over as I stared at the serene crystal-clear pool in the distance, imagining myself stretched out across a lawn chair with a book in one hand and a cold glass of lemonade in the other.

But before I could even turn the page of that relaxing book in my mind, my beautiful wife grabbed my shoulders, vigorously shook me out of my daydream, and pointed eagerly toward a brochure on the counter.

"Look honey, they have parasailing and jet skis and snorkeling! Oh, and this walking tour along the beach. I've always wanted us to try that! I'm sooooooo excited!!!"

I slowly looked down at the brochure and then back up at my wife's wide smile. All I wanted to do was relax and enjoy the view from our hotel room, but I quickly realized that God had very different plans in store for the two of us in sunny Cancun.

***

I undeniably and completely love my wife. But to be honest, we are complete opposites in many aspects. Where my introverted tendencies see an opportunity to rest in isolation and quietly enjoy the natural scenery with a book, her extroverted nature discovers underwater excursions, action-packed events, and outdoor activities for us to explore. Simply put, we think differently. We process experiences differently, have different perspectives on global issues, and have different views on the daily opportunities that enter our lives. But my wife and I are not unique. All of us, young and old, were created *differently* by God and have unique personalities. The world is *divinely diverse*.

Being divinely diverse means that God intentionally created everyone and everything on Earth to be different. Look at the very landscape of our planet. From one country to the next, you will easily find mountains, plains, beaches, and tropics. From the north to the south, you will find variations in climate and temperature, changes from snow to heat. From the east to the west, you will experience changes in season – from summer to winter, and from spring to fall.

As you explore further within each city and throughout every town, you will discover a variety of plants and animals. In fact, there are some species that are so small, they cannot even be seen with the naked eye. It is said that there are at least 5,416 different species of mammals, at least 10,000 species of birds, at least 18,000 species of fish, at least 391,000 species of plants, and at least 2 million species of insects.

Even more, we as the *human* species are divinely diverse. From home to home on every street, you will easily find diversity in ethnicity (Latinos, Africans, African Americans, Europeans, Asians, Middle Easterners, etc.), to diversity in culture and traditions, to diversity in customs and religion, to diversity in perspectives and opinions (yes, even on how best to vacation when in sunny Cancun). There are currently over 7.5 billion people living on planet Earth and yet no two people have the same fingerprints, not even twins. Everything and everyone around us is divinely diverse *by design*. But why would God make everything and everyone on Earth different?

In 1 Corinthians 1:12-27, the apostle Paul compares the body of Christ – the church – with the human body. The human body has many unique and distinct parts, both outward and inward, that each look and operate differently – the heart, the brain, the lungs, the legs. But when they all come together, they function as one unit to enable the human body to perform a wide range of tasks – walking, jumping, sitting, standing.

The members of the body do not argue with one another. The head does not envy the foot, and the heart does not debate the lung over its relative importance. Every part of the body carries out its unique function, however prominent or humble that function may be.

As it is in the human body, so should it also be in Christ's body, the church. Paul teaches us in 1 Corinthians 1:12-13 (NIV),

"Just as a body, though one, has many parts, but all its many parts form one body, so it is with Christ. For we were all baptized by one Spirit so as to form one body —

whether Jews or Gentiles, slave or free — and we were all given the one Spirit to drink."

Although we are all different, God still expects us to work together as a cohesive unit, much like our natural body. We should not compare ourselves to our neighbor, or envy our neighbor's gifts or opportunities, because we have all been assigned a different role in the body of Christ. Every task is critical to the church's overall health. Further, it is only when we all contribute to the body by completing our unique tasks to the best of our ability that the entire body of the church can function as it was designed by God.

Marriage works this way too. In Mark 10:8 (NLV), we learn that "the two are united into one." Each spouse — both husband and wife — are designed differently by God. But it is the *union* of those differences through the sacrament of marriage that makes the marital bond such a powerful force.

Husbands and wives are not called to be *uniform* or to act the same in every circumstance. Instead, they are called to walk together in *unity*. As such, they should not *compete* with one another. Instead, they should seek to *complement* each other in various ways, based upon their unique perspectives and giftings. While they may share the same mindset, goals, or core values that guide how they operate their marriage, they also must celebrate their unique differences, which ultimately dictate the roles they play on the team. In other words, while a husband and wife may be different, they must still operate as *one*.

In every relationship where God is given permission to dwell in the center, diversity does not subtract from the union. Instead, it adds. However, in order for a God-centered union to occur, one where diversity reinforces unity, there are three principles that every person must first learn about themselves and their partner. Every person seeking *unity in diversity* must learn that they are, by design, (1) divinely distinguished, (2) divinely deficient, and (3) divinely dependent.

Principle #1. Divinely Distinguished By Design

Two friends of ours, a married couple — let's call them John and Jane — were having a difficult time navigating a particularly troubling, yet common household chore —

washing the dishes. Both John and Jane had agreed that they would take turns washing the dishes and putting them away. However, John secretly hated doing the dishes. Whenever his turn arrived, John would avoid the kitchen like the plague until the sink began to pile up and sometimes even spill out onto the counter. Jane would become furious and constantly fuss with John until he finally got around to emptying the sink. Oddly, once John finished washing the dishes, he had no problem putting them away. In fact, he enjoyed placing the cups and plates in their proper place, perhaps due to a childhood fascination with puzzles and Lego blocks.

When Jane's turn came around to do the dishes, she wasted no time cleaning the bowls and silverware. As if cooking with a soap-filled sponge in her back pocket, the sink remained empty. However, when it came time to put the dry dishes away, Jane was often too busy cleaning something else to get to it. So, she procrastinated, and her clean dishes would pile up on the counter, much in the same way John's dirty dishes piled up in the sink. This time, John would fuss at Jane, pointing out that she was now the one making a mess and turning their lives upside down. John and Jane continued in this cycle, arguing over washing the dishes and putting the dishes away, every single day.

One day, after forgetting whose turn it was, they decided to do the dishes together. Jane happily agreed to wash, and John eagerly prepared to dry and organize the dishes into their proper places in the cabinet. For the first time, they laughed together and actually had fun doing the dishes. Even more, when they finished, not only were there no more dirty dishes piling up in the sink, there also were no more clean dishes stacked on the counter. Together, they were able to completely clean and put away everything.

***

The word "distinguished" is defined as being set apart based upon specific notable, or conspicuous characteristics. Have you ever asked someone, *"Do you know so and so?"* They probably responded with, *"How does he/she look?"* or *"Describe him/her to me."* You likely proceeded to describe the person based upon certain noticeable features or behaviors that distinguished them from others.

It might have been the color or texture of their hair, or the color of their eyes, or the color of their skin, or even their height or the way they talk. Whatever it may be, we tend to focus on *distinguishable* characteristics when we are identifying what makes one person stand out from the next.

The funny thing is, God makes this job easy for us. God created all of us to stand out by our distinguishable characteristics. In other words, each of us is a designer's original. However, we are not only distinguishable by our physical features. We also are distinguished by what God has placed on the inside of us.

The Bible declares in Psalms 139:14 (KJV),

> *"I will praise thee; for I am fearfully and wonderfully made: marvelous are thy works; and that my soul knoweth right well."*

The first step toward understanding that you are divinely distinguished is learning to celebrate *who* God made you to be. You and I are "marvelous works" of the Creator of the universe. We are not mistakes, misfits, or mishaps. God designed us *on* purpose and filled us *with* purpose.

We each have *different* gifts, *different* ideas, and *different* perspectives. But these differences, when aligned together based upon our *same* goals, *same* objectives, and *same* desired outcomes, position us to win the game. Like the players of a football team, we come in different shapes and sizes with different skills and abilities. But together, we form an unstoppable unit.

We see this concept play out in the body of Christ during Sunday service. Take the choir as one example. A choir is comprised of individuals who are distinguishable by their musical voice. Further, every section of the choir is comprised of singers who are distinguishable by their unique abilities to sing in a different range or key. Sometimes, different members of the choir, such as soloists, are further distinguished and singled out during the song. But when they all come together in unity, the members of the choir make beautiful music.

The same can be said for the marital relationship, where differences abound. The wife has certain characteristics and skills that the husband does not possess, and the husband has certain characteristics and skills that the wife does not possess. Although they do not have the same opinions or perspectives, they have the same core values and the same driving goal – to become a living representation of the love of Jesus Christ.

The second step toward understanding that you are divinely distinguished is realizing that God planned it that way. The Bible teaches us in 1 Corinthians 12:18 (MSG):

"As it is, we see that God has carefully placed each part of the body right where he wanted it."

God has placed you right where he wants you to be. Do not despise how God designed you. Do not envy the gifts or talents of that coworker on your job, or that college roommate who is a success. God uniquely equipped you with gifts, talents, opinions, perspectives, and personality to be a gift to someone else. Yes, a wife is in fact a gift to her husband, and a husband is a gift to his wife. She supplies what is missing in his life to help him achieve his purpose in the body of Christ, and he does the same for her.

Principle #2. Divinely Deficient By Design

Adam was God's main man. Made in God's image and likeness, he was given the power to simply see an animal and name it. In fact, Adam named *all* of the animals – lions, tigers, bears . . . the list goes on. Given the great diversity of species on our planet, this alone was an incredible ability and an awesome accomplishment. Most of us today have trouble remembering the names of our many online friends. Nevertheless, although Adam was able to accomplish an extraordinary feat, God designed him to be deficient in some aspects of his life and observed that the man needed some help.

In Genesis 2:18 (KJV), the Bible declares,

"And the LORD God said, It is not good that the man should be alone; I will make him an help meet for him."

Accordingly, God created the woman – Eve – to complement Adam. Eve was not created to *compete* with Adam. Rather, Eve was created to *complement* Adam. Eve possessed certain distinguishable gifts that Adam did not have, and Adam possessed certain distinguishable gifts that Eve did not have. God gave Adam exactly who he needed to help him accomplish God's purpose for his life.

***

The word "deficient" is defined as lacking in an area of importance. God does not design us to live independent and self-sufficient lives. Instead, he crafts us as *deficient* beings, requiring us to form intentional relationships with others – in *unity* – as we seek to fulfill our purpose. Unity is how we *co-operate* with God – embracing who God has called us to be *and* celebrating others as they operate in their unique calling. The gifts that He didn't give to me, He may have given to you. The gifts that He didn't give to you, He may have given to me or to someone else. As the body of Christ, it is our job to recognize that we need one another's *imperfect* parts to live healthy and *whole* lives together.

The first step toward better understanding why we are deficient by design is recognizing that God doesn't give everyone the same gifts. In Ephesians 2:10 (KGV), the Bible declares,

> *"For we are his workmanship, created in Christ Jesus unto good works, which God hath before ordained that we should walk in them."*

God has ordained each of us to accomplish a specific task during our walk on Earth. This task, our *purpose*, is custom-made for you and for me. In other words, we are God's fabric, and He is the master tailor, crafting a unique workmanship that matches our role in the body of Christ. In addition to giving us purpose – a custom-made "outfit" or role in the body of Christ (1 Corinthians 12:28), God equips each of us with the specific tools necessary to help us accomplish that purpose. These tools in our toolbelt are our spiritual gifts.

Romans 12:6-8 (NIV) explains,

"We have different gifts, according to the grace given to each of us. If your gift is prophesying, then prophesy in accordance with your faith; if it is serving, then serve; if it is teaching, then teach; if it is to encourage, then give encouragement; if it is giving, then give generously; if it is to lead, do it diligently; if it is to show mercy, do it cheerfully."

The second step toward better understanding why we are deficient by design is realizing that we need one another to fulfill our assignment. The foot cannot fulfill its assignment in the body unless it is connected to a leg. A chopped-off foot left alone to fend for itself in the field will never fulfill its God-given function to help the body reach a goal. Likewise, we need one another.

Our spiritual gifts are tools to build with, not toys to play with or weapons to fight with. And while we can play alone or even fight by ourselves, no one ever built a sturdy and solid house alone. The anointing of Christ flows when we operate in our God-given purpose and use our God-given gifts while working together as a team.

This does *not* mean that we will never make mistakes when we are operating in our purpose or using our spiritual gifts. We all fall short of God's glory and we all continue along our path but for the amazing grace of Jesus Christ. But it *does* mean that you are *not* a mistake. Rather, you are a necessary gift to the body of Christ. You are an answer to a problem in your community. You are a solution to the puzzle of God's awesome purpose for your local church. You are a source of inspiration for a doubting parent, and a beacon of light in a world hungry for hope. You are divinely deficient.

Principle #3. Divinely Dependent By Design

From time to time, my wife and I watch live football together at FedExField in

Washington, D.C. We love sitting in the stadium and munching on hot dogs while we cheer for our favorite team. While she loves the general energy and excitement of the game, I am often much more focused on the specific plays taking place down on the field.

Turning toward my wife, lost in the details of the game, I might easily find myself saying something like,

> *"The quarterback just received the snap, faked the handoff to the halfback who ran directly toward the line of scrimmage, and then tossed the ball laterally to the fullback as he made his way toward the sideline. Did they really think that would work?"*

Although a conversation about football strategy with my wife is unlikely to follow, these moments remind me that God-centered relationships are often just like football.

On the football field, all the players need one another to be successful. The quarterback cannot be a quarterback by himself. He needs a tailback to run with the ball after a pitch, he needs a wide receiver to catch the ball after a throw, and he *definitely* needs linemen to block the other team before a play-ending tackle. It is only within the context of the *team* that the quarterback can be effective. In fact, if there is no team, then there can be no quarterback.

Likewise, a husband cannot be a husband by himself. A wife cannot be a wife by herself. Each spouse is dependent on the other to *be* who they are called to be in marriage.

***

The word "dependent" is defined as relying on someone or something for support or aid. God intends for us to work together to accomplish the purpose that he has set out before us. One of the biggest challenges facing many purpose-driven individuals today is that they try to accomplish their vision on their own. We are intentionally designed by God to be mutually dependent on one another as we seek to build the kingdom. To put it simply, no preacher ever sustained a church without church members.

The Bible teaches us in Romans 12:5 (AMP),

> *"so we, who are many, are [nevertheless just] one body in Christ, and individually [we are] parts one of another [mutually dependent on each other]."*

One of the primary reasons why we are *dependent* by design is because *you* cannot see *you*. We need like-minded individuals by our side – our teammates – to help us navigate the game of life toward the end goal of our purpose. Our teammates help us navigate the field, help block opponents coming our way when we are facing the other direction, and help remind us when we are veering away from the playbook.

As believers, this means finding like-minded individuals who can help us remain committed to the values of Christ, pray with and for us when unexpected challenges come our way, and encourage us to return to the principles of scripture when we veer off course.

As the Bible declares in Ecclesiastes 4:9,

"Two are better than one, because they have a good return for their labor."

Additionally, we also need someone – a coach – to help us become better at the game. A coach is someone outside of yourself who observes how you play to help you become a better you. Whether by pointing out your flaws or teaching you how to grow beyond your mistakes, a coach shows you the parts of you that you cannot see.

As believers, we find our teammates when we join a church and get involved in ministry groups. In marriage, we find a teammate in our spouse. But during the game of life, with our team by our side, we must rely on the teachings of Jesus Christ, whether taught through Bible study or counseling or during weekly Sunday sermons, to help "coach" us towards improving how we play.

You cannot win the game alone. In marriage, you partner with a teammate who commits to playing the same game, but who also brings different talents to the field and plays a different position. For those who are single or may not be called to the ministry of marriage, it is still important to surround yourself with a team of like-minded individuals – a church community – who can help you navigate the field toward purpose.

In both cases, with the Bible as your playbook, and Jesus Christ as your coach, you will never be defeated.

2

Marriage is W.O.R.K.

" A great marriage isn't something that just happens; it's something that must be created."

~ Fawn Weaver

There are many definitions and many different perceptions of marriage. My wife and I believe that marriage is the joining of a man and woman in a covenant relationship with God for the central purpose of representing to the world the love of Jesus Christ for His bride, the Church. This union is both a life-long journey and a serious personal commitment that involves W.O.R.K. Some of you may be asking,

"What does the mnemonic W.O.R.K. represent?"

As I will soon explain, each letter in the word W.O.R.K. represents an important habit that both a husband and wife must learn to build a successful and long-lasting marriage.

Habit #1. Willing to conform to the image of Christ.

If you want to build a successful and lasting marriage, or if you desire healthy and thriving relationships, then you must be *willing* to conform to the image of Jesus Christ and not to the images of success or happiness defined by the world.

The Bible declares in Romans 12:2 (KJV),

> *"And be not conformed to this world, but be ye transformed by the renewing of your mind, that ye may prove what is that good, and acceptable, and perfect, will of God.*

The word *conform* means to put on the appearance, or to put on the form or fashion of another person or thing. We should not put on the habits, behaviors, customs, and toxic mindsets of this world. Instead, the writer of the book of Romans teaches us that in everything we do, we should put on the appearance or the form of the Word of God. This includes our marriage and our relationships.

Biblical marriage is *spiritual*, not physical. That is why so many people today struggle in marriage. They approach it with a carnal mind, focusing on how their spouse makes them feel *physically*, rather than how their spouse helps them grow *spiritually*. When we view marriage through a worldly perspective focused on our feelings, it seems unnatural to sacrifice for another person for a lifetime because we know it will not always feel good.

These sacrifices and the many others that are required within a successful marital relationship require spiritual maturity. Many people enter marriage with unhealthy and unstable expectations that are shaped by the many examples they observed in the home or in their community. Media also plays a significant role in the formation of our expectations regarding marriage.

Many television programs and movies do not depict a realistic view of marriage. Some of the women on the Real Housewives reality shows are not even married! The truth is that reality shows aren't reality at all. They are scripted programs designed to boost viewership and generate ratings. Unfortunately, many people bring these unrealistic expectations into the marriage relationship.

Why? Simply put, their expectations and opinions about marriage are shaped by the *world* and not by the *Word* of God.

Is your marriage conforming to the Kingdom of God or the kingdom of darkness? Are your beliefs and behaviors aligned with God or with the world? Is transformation occurring in you and in your marriage?

Transformation is not a change from the outside in, but a change from the inside out. Take the caterpillar as an example. The caterpillar goes into a cocoon, and over a period of time, transforms into a beautiful butterfly. Caterpillar before; butterfly after. There is a total transformation. It simply doesn't look the same.

That is exactly what God wants to do in our lives. Allow God to transform your marriage to the point where it doesn't look the same after. He can take your marriage from the caterpillar stage to the butterfly stage if you let Him.

The Bible says that we are to transform our mind. How do we transform our mind? The Bible explains that transformation occurs by the *renewing* of your mind. Renewing means to renovate. It means to make anew, to refresh, to revive, to restore, to repair, to return something to good or better condition. Putting it in the language of today's modern digital age, it means to *reboot*.

When your computer is not functioning properly, the first thing that they often tell you to do is reboot. Hold down the power button and start it all over again. Likewise, when your marriage is not functioning properly, or if your marriage is not on key with God, you need to reboot your mind. You need to go back to the owner's manual, which is the Word of God, and refresh, revive, restore, repair, *reboot* your mind according to God's Word.

The process of rebooting your mind is a process of renovation. When you renovate any structure, whether it's a building or a house, you take out the old and you put in the new. That's what we need to do to our minds. We need to take out the old mentality and replace it with a new mentality. We need to put in fresh thinking, and fresh thinking comes from the Word of God.

Colossians 3:10 (NIV) tells us

"and have put on the new self, which is being renewed in knowledge in the image of its Creator."

Ephesians 4:23 (KJV) says,

"And be renewed in the spirit of your mind."

Renewing your mind is an intentional and continual process. However, renewing of the mind does not just happen all at once, nor is it a one-time event. It is a constant exercise of rebooting your mind, starting over again and again, and learning from your mistakes. When you reboot your mind by learning from your mistakes, you produce a change in your attitude, and ultimately, a transformation in your behavior. You become that beautiful butterfly who was once hidden in a cocoon.

Habit #2. Open to giving your spouse what they need.

When I attended North Carolina A & T University for college, I majored in Industrial Engineering. Although most of my courses were in the field of science and engineering, I also took some optional elective courses. But, for me to graduate, I had to complete the required courses in my engineering department, which was my primary area of focus.

Some of you may have majored in other fields of study like Biology, Psychology or Sociology. Well believe it or not, I am still in school today. Before you call me an overachiever or bookworm, let me explain. See, now I have a new major. My new course of study is *Bobette-ology*. That's my major. My primary area of focus is on studying my spouse. In order for me to give my wife what she needs, I must study her, investigate her, ask her questions, and take detailed notes in my mental notebook.

You were crafted and created to fulfill certain needs in the life of your spouse, needs that no one else is authorized to fulfill. Jimmy Evans explains in his book, *Marriage on the Rock*, that a wife has four primary needs:

(1) security;

(2) non-sexual touch;

(3) open and honest communication; and

(4) leadership.

Jimmy Evans also explains that the needs of a husband are:

(1) sexual fulfillment;

(2) honor/respect;

(3) recreational companionship; and

(4) domestic support.

Whether you are a husband or a wife, make a commitment to fill your spouse's love tank by meeting their needs. Intentionally make regular deposits into their tank. Husbands, find ways to demonstrate leadership and security to your wife through open and honest conversations about your hopes and dreams for the family. Wives, find ways to communicate honor and respect to your husband by supporting their vision and being a companion for some of their recreational hobbies. Remember, marriage is W.O.R.K.!

In his book, *The Five Love Languages*, Dr. Gary Chapman explains that there are 5 love languages:

(1) acts of service;

(2) physical touch;

(3) quality time;

(4) words of affirmation; and

(5) gifts.

Dr. Chapman further explains that everyone has a primary love language. Sometimes we make the mistake of communicating *our* love language to our spouse instead of speaking *their* love language. This can cause confusion and frustration.

After reading Dr. Chapman's book, I asked my wife, *"What is your primary love language?"* She quickly responded, *"All of them!"* I said, *"That can't be!"*

So, I began to observe her more closely and pulled out my mental notebook. I listened intently to what my wife had to say. I asked her about her likes and dislikes, and her favorite things to do. I put myself back in study mode. And soon enough, I discovered that her primary love language is quality time.

It does not matter to my wife what we are doing, as long we are doing it together. There are times when we are doing nothing, and she is ok with that, as long as we are together. Being together and having intimate conversation fills her love tank to the brim.

Do you know your spouse's love language?

If not, find out what it is and begin communicating to him or her in their language of love.

Lastly, it is important to remain open to receiving constructive criticism from your spouse. I know it's not easy to hear constructive criticism from your spouse, but it is necessary. Quite honestly, constructive criticism is a gift because it can help you become a better you. Be open to what your spouse has to say about you.

On the other hand, when giving constructive criticism, make sure that it is **_constructive_** and not destructive. We must speak the truth in love. In other words, your reason for addressing the issue is to help your spouse, not to hurt them. Your purpose for discussing it is to build up, not to tear down.

If the criticism is going to tear down your spouse and not build them up, then maybe you shouldn't say it at all. If what you are planning to say does not give life, then maybe you should keep those words buried in your mental grave. Your words are powerful. Every day, you have the opportunity to influence and shape your spouse with the words you speak. Use them wisely.

As Proverbs 18:21(KJV) teaches us,

"Death and life are in the power of the tongue: And they that love it shall eat the fruit thereof."

Habit #3. Ready to protect and defend the sanctity of your marital relationship.

The word *ready* means to be completely prepared or in fit condition for immediate action or use. Remember, you are in a battle. You must be prepared to fight on a moment's notice. No one, whether they are interacting with you in the flesh or virtually on the internet, should take the place of your spouse in your heart and in your thoughts.

In Matthew 5:28 (NIV), Jesus says,

"But I tell you that anyone who looks at a woman lustfully has already committed adultery with her in his heart."

This is important. Be ready. Nobody else should be first. No one should take the place of your spouse. Not in your heart, not in your thoughts, not in your compliments, and not in your actions. Do not allow yourself to leave the house and "forget" to say goodbye to your spouse, but once you arrive at work, "remember" to remind your fellow co-worker how wonderful he/she looks and how good he/she smells. Don't be ignorant of the enemy's devices.

***

What are some practical methods of protecting and defending the sacredness of your marital relationship?

First, do not meditate on any negative thoughts of your spouse.

Acknowledge the thoughts, discuss them, and exchange them with positive intentions. Focus on the right things that your spouse is doing and verbally acknowledge them.

Second, do not compare.

It will be easier to focus on positive thoughts of your spouse by not comparing your spouse with other men or women. God designed your spouse just for you, so keep your eyes on the prize.

Third, become a part of the solution and not the problem.

Be willing to help your spouse become better. If he/she is trying to lose weight, work out with them. If he/she is attending a support group for an addiction, go with them to the meeting. Become a listening ear when they need to vent.

Husband and wife, you are on the same team! You are not each other's enemy. The enemy is Satan. Satan would like for you to think that your spouse is the enemy. But you are "mates!" Partners in marriage, partners *IN* life and partners *FOR* life!

Teammates, whether they win or lose, are in it together. Classmates learn and study together. Playmates play together, enjoy life together, travel together, and vacation together. Cellmates go through hard times and difficult seasons together. Soul mates are joined together, and nothing and nobody can separate them. Allow your spouse to be your mate!

Fourth, you must guard your gates.

Gates are points of entry. The points of entry to your heart and mind are your ears and eyes. You must guard your *ear*-gates and your *eye*-gates with all diligence! Be selective about what you watch and who you listen to.

Listen husbands and single brothers — men are stimulated by what and whom we see. That is why pornography is a billion-dollar business. But pornography will destroy your family, your influence, and your life. Here are just a few statistics:

*There are 26 million pornographic websites.

*According to the research, approximately 64 percent, or two thirds of U.S. men admit to viewing porn at least monthly, with the number of Christian men nearly equal to the national average.

*Eight out of ten (79%) men between the ages of 18 and 30 view pornography at least monthly.

*Two thirds (67%) of men between the ages of 31 and 49 view pornography at least monthly.

*One half of men between 50 and 68 views porn monthly.

When sexually aroused by pornographic images, several hormones are released in your brain. One is a hormone called *epinephrine*. When epinephrine is released, the image you are viewing is permanently burned into your memory. This is why a pornographic image viewed years ago remains in your memory as if you saw it yesterday.

Some husbands want their wives to act out the scenes that they have buried in their minds. They want their wife to perform sexually what they have seen on TV or on their computer screen. Husband, your wife cannot compete with the images in your mind. You must protect and defend the purity of your marriage.

Fifth, you must hold yourself accountability by joining a community.

One of the ways to protect and defend the purity of your marriage is to surround yourself with a community of likeminded men (for husbands) and women (for wives) who will hold you accountable.

As Proverbs 11:1(AMP) says,

"Where there is no [wise, intelligent] guidance, the people fall [and go off course like a ship without a helm], But in the abundance of [wise and godly] counselors

there is victory."

There are some women who feel that they are not being appreciated in their relationship. They feel that they're not being accepted by their partner, or that they're not being loved. They may even feel that they are not getting the emotional support that they need. *He doesn't talk to me, that's why I don't talk to him.*

You must protect the sacredness of your marriage. If your husband is not giving you what you need, that is not a reason to give up on marriage. All lasting relationships require commitment and communication. If you have tried it and it's not working, keep working at it. As James teaches us, the effectual fervent prayers of righteous people avail much. (James 5:16 KJV)

Keep praying and keep talking. Keep believing, keep rebuking, and keep binding the hands of the enemy. You've got to do it. If you need help, get help. If you need support, get support. You can even have someone mediate as you and your spouse talk to one another so that you can begin to listen to one another.

This does not mean that you should not maintain your privacy. There shouldn't be any sharing of intimate details or feelings with someone who is not your spouse. If you're sharing any intimate details of your marriage, or if you are sharing intimate feelings about your marriage, make sure it is only with a trusted advisor that you both have chosen, not someone on your job or another person in the church.

You should not be sharing your frustrations with Sister Renee on the choir. You should not be sharing your doubts with Brother John in the cubicle next to you. That is setting yourself up for a fall and not protecting the sacredness and purity of your marriage.

As Job 31:1 (MSG) declares,

"I made a solemn pact with myself never to undress a girl with my eyes"

Brothers, husbands, want-to-be husbands, make a covenant with your eyes that you will not undress your sister, because that's who she is. She is your sister.

Habit #4. Keeping the flames of passion and romance burning.

The final letter in W.O.R.K. stands for *Keeping the flames of passion and romance burning.* Listen, it's not going to just happen. You must be intentional. If you pursued her before you got married, you've still got to pursue her after you say *I do.* Hear me husbands, you must date your wife. Hear me wives, you must date your husbands. If you dressed up for him before you got married, continue to look cute for him after the wedding bells toll.

Instead of looking for ways to fulfill a temporary desire based on the illusion of greener pastures, find lasting *pleasure.* This is what God wants you to do. God wants you to find pleasure and happiness in the relationship that he gave you. He gave you *this* relationship.

I love it when Solomon wisely says in Proverbs 5:15 (NIV),

"Drink water from your own cistern, running water from your own well."

That's good advice. Drink from your own cistern. There is fresh water there. Wife, there is a new man inside of your husband. Husband, there's a new woman inside of your wife. Are you woman or man enough to get it out and drink from the well God gave you?

Keep the flames of passion and romance burning. Romance is derived from the same root word as *encourage*. It means to come alongside. When you romance your spouse, what you are saying to him or her is that you are worth the time and the expense. Romance communicates to your spouse that you care about them.

Make time for romance and *invest* in your romance. Early on in our marriage, we didn't have a lot of money. My wife and I lived in a one-bedroom apartment. At that time, the utilities were included in the rent. The ceiling in our bedroom was white and covered with little sparkles. If you turned off the lights and shined a flashlight at the ceiling, it looked like stars in the nighttime sky.

So, sometimes we would turn the heat up, turn off the lights, lie in bed, and shine a flashlight on the ceiling while pretending that we were on a beach on a Caribbean island looking up at the stars. We would talk about our dreams and our future life together.

Husbands and wives, don't stop dreaming. Don't stop believing in your vision. Share your hearts with one another. When you do, the flames will burn brightly. Part of keeping the flames of passion and romance burning is having a scheduled date night on your calendar. Go places that you both enjoy such as the movies or the park. You can even book an overnight stay at a local hotel. Believe me, it will bring a fresh look and a new outlook to your relationship.

As Pastor Mark Batterson says,

"Change of place plus change of pace equals change of perspective."

When you change the place – getting away from the house and staying at a local hotel for one night – and change your pace –

slowing down from your hectic work schedule and enjoying your spouse – things begin to change. In life, we are often running so fast that we pass one another by. Both the husband and wife are working. Or one spouse is working long hours while the other stays at home. With so much going on in life, if you're not careful, you may lose the connection and allow the flames to grow dim.

You need to slow down and change the place. Get out of the house. Go to the beach. Take a weekend vacation. Drive somewhere just to see something new. Change your place, but also remember to change your pace. Slowing down allows you to develop a change in your perspective. When you change your place and change your pace, it gives you a fresh outlook and a new perspective on the gift of marriage and the blessing of having *your* spouse. It will give you the opportunity to reconnect and keep those flames of passion and romance burning bright.

3

I L.O.V.E. You

" Where there is love, there is life."

~ Mahatma Gandhi

I absolutely love my husband. But we all know that love is not easy. The apostle Paul, in 1 Corinithians 13:4-8 (NLT) sounds the alarm for us as he eagerly attempts to help us gain a deeper understanding of love. He wrote:

"Love is patient and kind. Love is not jealous or boastful or proud or rude. It does not demand its own way. It is not irritable, and it keeps no record of being wronged. It does not rejoice about injustice but rejoices whenever the truth wins out. Love never gives up, never loses faith, is always hopeful, and endures through every circumstance."

Let's be honest about the marriage covenant. Without a doubt, there are some **big** challenges that commonly afflict marital relationships, none of which are going anywhere anytime soon. You already know the kinds of challenges that I am talking about – communication, blended families, in-laws, and financial struggles, to name just a few. Here's one that has destroyed countless marriages — *lust*. I'm not talking about lust for your spouse. I am talking about lust for *other* people and *other* things outside of the home.

We live in a highly sexualized society that delivers a constant and alluring drumbeat of distractions. As Paul teaches us in 1 John 2:16 (NIV):

> *"the lust of the eye, the lust of the flesh, and the pride of life — comes not from the Father but from the world."*

Lust comes not from God, but as a result of our unregenerate, human and sinful nature. It is further inflamed by the books we read, the TV shows and movies we watch, and the people we surround ourselves with, each and every day. One statement that I hear often from my husband, and it continues to ring true today, is

> *"there is a big different between love and lust. Love is fulfilling the need of another at your expense. Lust is fulfilling your desire at the expense of another."*

Lust is an altered state of consciousness. Studies reveal that the brain, when in a state of lust, is much like a brain on drugs. MRI scans have shown that the same area in the brain that lights up when a drug addict gets a fix of cocaine is the same area that lights up when a person is experiencing the intense *lust* of physical attraction. Pure lust is based solely on nothing other than physical attraction and fantasy, and it often dissipates when the "real person" surfaces.

Despite the presence of big challenges like lust that distract us from God's plan for our lives, often it is the small *petty* problems that destabilize the love in our relationships. Do you know what I am talking about? You know, those small quirks and annoying habits that get on your "reserved" nerve (that's one past the "last nerve").

The dirty socks on the floor. The way your spouse chews so loud that you are worried the neighbors might start to complain. The relentless drip of that faucet after they rush out of the bathroom yet again without fully turning the knob closed. These tiny quirks and bothersome behaviors, little by little over time, may begin to erode the goodwill that underlies our relationships. Before you know it, you begin to feel unloved, unheard, and underappreciated.

Why does he text and keep checking his phone during dinner? Why won't she squeeze the toothpaste from the bottom? Why does he have the TV up so loud, and why is it still on even though the game is over?

Even worse, when we voice our opinions, not only do we fail to see any change in their behavior, but *they* begin to feel criticized and controlled. Intimacy eventually becomes a fading memory.

The Bible explains the danger of focusing too much on our spouse's quirks and not enough on *our* response.

Proverbs 19:13 (NIV) says,

". . . a quarrelsome [nagging] wife is like the constant dripping of a leaky roof."

A part of loving your spouse is learning that irritations are inevitable in all relationships. It's simply not possible to find another human on this Earth whose every quirk, habit, and personal preference perfectly aligns with yours. You must learn to love your imperfect spouse in the same way that Christ loves you.

Ephesians 5:25 (MSG) teaches us,

"Husbands, go all out in your love for your wives, exactly as Christ did for the church — a love marked by giving, not getting."

According to Maslow's hierarchy of needs, we all have five primary needs: (1) physiological needs; (2) safety needs; (3) the need for love and belonging; (4) the need for esteem; and (5) the need for self-actualization.

Which one of these needs is most important? According to Psychology Today, "Love is the most profound emotion known to human beings." We see this reflected in popular culture as well. What are the highest grossing movies in the U.S.? Number 2 on the list is *Avatar* (2009) with approximately $760,500,000 in gross revenues, and number 5 is the classic movie *Titanic* (1997) with approximately $659,300,00 in gross revenue. The common thread in both of these movies is that the main characters met, and they fell in LOVE.

As Jesus revealed in Matthew 22:36-40 (KJV),

"Master, which is the great commandment in the law? Jesus said unto him, Thou shalt love the Lord thy God with all thy heart, and with all thy soul, and with all thy mind. This is the first and great commandment. And the second is like unto it, Thou shalt love thy neighbor as thyself. On these two commandments hang all the law and the prophets."

For many people, romantic relationships are the most meaningful aspect of their lives. But the ability to have a healthy, loving, and long-lasting relationship is not something that is instinctual. We learn how to develop and sustain healthy relationships from God, through our experiences, and by living in community with one another.

The first thing we must understand is that love is a triangle. Love has three sides: (1) *Eros*, which is the physical side of the triangle, represented by passionate and sexual love; (2) *Phileo*, which is the emotional side of the triangle, represented by our fond affections for our friends; and (3) *Agape*, which is the spiritual side of the love triangle, the base of the triangle, represented by an unconditional and self-sacrificing love that is independent of the object being loved.

The Bible explains in 1 Corinthians 13:4-8 (MSG),

> *"Love never gives up. Love cares more for others than for self. Love doesn't want what it doesn't have. Love doesn't strut, Doesn't have a swelled head, Doesn't force itself on others, Isn't always "me first,"*

Doesn't fly off the handle, Doesn't keep score of the sins of others, Doesn't revel when others grovel, Takes pleasure in the flowering of truth, Puts up with anything, Trusts God always, Always looks for the best, Never looks back, But keeps going to the end. Love never dies."

This is further exemplified by the story of Jacob and Rachel in Genesis 29:20 (NIV), which says,

"So Jacob served seven years to get Rachel, but they seemed like only a few days to him because of his love for her."

Almost all of us have experienced a failed relationship or two. As a result, most of us must work diligently, each and every day, to master the skills necessary to make the relationships we have left flourish. The good news is that with effort and perseverance, you can learn how to implement the key strategies that my husband and I use in our marriage that have enabled our relationship to last.

I L. O. V. E. You

There are four strategies that Cedric and I have implemented in our marriage that have helped us to strengthen the love that we have for one another.

Strategy #1 – I Listen to You

First, I **Listen** to my husband. I pay close attention to what he is saying, through his words, eyes, and through his actions. There is a big difference between hearing someone and listening to someone. Hearing is physiological, the ability to perceive sounds that are caused by vibrations inside of the ear. Listening is so much more, an intellectual devotion to what the ear is picking up from those traveling sound waves. In other words, hearing is involuntary, while listening is voluntary.

Listening is intentional. Listening is also a process. It is possible to hear someone and not listen to them. If you live near a busy street, the noise may be annoying at first, but soon enough you learn how to tune *out* the noise and tune *in* to the other things or people around you.

It's very difficult to hide the fact that you're not listening to your spouse. He or she will figure it out sooner or later. And, if it becomes a regular occurrence, they may learn to save their words for someone who will really listen.

Listening not only involves your ears, but also your eyes and your body. I know what you are saying. *Lady Bobette, what are you talking about? My eyes and body?!* Let me explain. Next time you are talking to someone, take a moment to notice their body posture. Are their arms or legs crossed? Are they facing you, or turned away? Are they looking at you, or staring off into outer space or at the sports game on TV?

It is equally as important to make eye contact with your spouse when you are having a conversation as it is to actually process what they are saying. Wandering eyes lead to a wandering mind. This doesn't mean that you should creep them out with an unblinking stare. Still, make sure that your spouse is the center of your attention when you are talking to them. This means turning off the TV, putting down your phone, and focusing on the words coming out of their mouth.

To ensure that your spouse knows that you are listening, it helps to ask questions about what is being said. Try not to interrupt them. Instead, make appropriate and timely comments that allow you to dig deeper into the conversation.

As the Bible affirms in James 1:19 (MSG),

> *"Post this at all the intersections, dear friends: Lead with your ears, follow up with your tongue, and let anger straggle along in the rear."*

Strategy #2 – I Observe You

Second, I **Observe** my husband. I watch him steadily and consider carefully his actions and behaviors. I look to him and I attend to him.

To put it simply, I *study* my spouse. Wives and husbands, you must learn your spouse's likes and dislikes. Learn their list of "favorites" – their favorite color, food, song, time of the year, hobby, etc. Your goal should be to learn their moods, temperament, and personality for every season of the year (and please know it may change over the years). But (*and this is key*) if you don't know, ask questions. You will never learn the answers to the questions you don't ask.

Proverbs 31:26 (MSG) tells us,

"When she speaks she has something worthwhile to say, and she always says it kindly."

Observe also means to keep safe, to protect, to watch over, and to guard (*i.e. watch each other's back!*) Don't leave your spouse uncovered!

Cover your spouse with prayer and fasting. By praying for them, you supply a need that only you are called to meet. Even more, you should inform your spouse about people who have an affection for them. That's right ladies. Tell your husband when you discover that another woman has a thing for his smile, talk, or physique. How do you do it? Simple - *"Honey, I think she likes you."* That's it! And gentlemen, you need to do the same!

In the book of Genesis in chapter 16, Sarah sends Hagar (her handmaiden) to sleep with Abraham so that they can have a son. Sarah did not trust in God's promise and pray for her husband's leadership during their time of hardship. Sarah did not cover Abraham.

Later in Genesis in chapter 20, Abraham tells Abimelech that Sarah was his sister. Abraham did not cover Sarah. He did not trust God and honor his wife's role in his life. Instead, he gave in to his fears and lied. You need to cover your spouse.

Strategy #3 – I Value You

Third, I **Value** my husband. To value your spouse means to regard or esteem them highly. Another word for value is HONOR. Husbands are commanded to honor, or *value* their wives.

According to 1 Peter 3:7 (AMP)

"In the same way, you husbands, live with your wives in an understanding way [with

great gentleness and tact, and with an intelligent regard for the marriage relationship], as with [a]someone physically weaker, since she is a woman. Show her honor and respect as a fellow heir of the grace of life, so that your prayers will not be hindered or ineffective."

When the Bible says "weaker vessel" it does not mean that the woman is frail or intellectually inferior. Instead, it means that she is more tender and delicate than a man. A woman should be regarded and treated with special kindness and attention by her spouse.

The first thing God said when He created the woman was that she was designed to be a helpmeet to her husband — a companion, protector, source of aid, and supporter. Married women can get so busy with other things, including their children, that they forget that their *first* calling is to be a wife.

Women, you are called to be by your husband's side. That's where you were taken from.

How often are you by your husband's side?

If you don't see a wife near her husband, what do you often think? What does that communicate to you? If your first thought is that she must not want to be around him, or that she does not have a very close relationship with him, then what do you think your absence from your husband's life communicates to your community, church, or work place?

It is very hard for someone else to try to be by your husband's side when you already occupy that position. Keep in mind, your husband's world may encompass more than his home, ministry assignment, and place of employment.

A man's two most important needs in establishing his sense of self-worth is respect and sexual intimacy with his wife. Wife, you are the only biblically authorized woman to fulfill his sexual needs. As wives, we honor our husband by submitting (willfully yielding) to his leadership.

The Bible declares in 1 Peter 3:1 (KJV),

"Likewise, ye wives, be in subjection to your own husbands; that, if any obey not the word, they also may without the word be won by the conversation of the wives."

When you value your spouse, what you REALLY are saying is *You are important to me, and whatever is important to you is important to me!*

Do not value another person or thing more than your spouse! Why are you giving another person a compliment when you haven't even applauded your spouse? Why are you devoting more time to ministry than to your spouse? What about your children, job, friends, or other family members? Are you putting them first?

Your spouse should be numero uno! Not your mom or your dad, not your sister or your brother, not your pastor, not your best friend, not even your children. After God, your spouse is your first priority.

Genesis 2:24 (KJV) commands us,

"Therefore, shall a man leave his father and his mother, and shall cleave unto his wife: and they shall be one flesh."

Don't give the best of yourself to others. Give it to your spouse. What is your best? Is it your ability to talk? Are you an excellent listener? Do you get dressed up for the office or church, but don't desire to dress nice for your spouse?

How we speak to our spouse communicates how much we value him or her. Be careful not to focus on who you desire for your spouse to become, but instead appreciate them for where they are today on the journey of self-development and growth.

Wives, call your husband a mighty man of valor! Affirm and encourage him. Husbands, speak into existence that your wife is a virtuous woman! God honors us by calling us by our "name" – the things that He knows we shall become. You should do the same!

Strategy #4 – I Embrace You

Finally, I **Embrace** my husband. This is where you make the decision to either accept your spouse's uniqueness or see it as a character flaw that aggravates you. I am not referring to behaviors that can be changed. I am referring to temperament, personality, and the core of who he or she is.

I am an extrovert. I enjoy talking to and meeting people. My husband on the other hand is an introvert. He is far more comfortable with one-on-one interaction. Now, that doesn't mean that he doesn't like people or always avoids crowds. Nor does it mean that I cannot have a meaningful one-on-one conversation with one person. I am sure there are times when my husband would like me to talk less, and there are certainly times when I want my husband to talk more. We have both learned to accept one another for who we are, and as a result, we've also learned from each other. It's a balancing act.

You either embrace your spouse as someone who complements you, or you decide that they're simply someone who you have to tolerate for the rest of your life. You may find yourself saying things like, *"I don't know if I can take this."* Yet, it is right here and right now, at this very point in your life, when kids, work, friends, hot flashes PMS, hormones, and everything else that you must balance, will determine the future of your marital relationship.

Embracing your spouse requires intentionality and communication. Who will handle the housework and who does the yard work? Who's going to change the oil and put gas in the car? Who's going to take out the trash? Who's getting up at 3:00 a.m. to feed and change the baby? How will we handle disciplining and setting parameters for the children? These are all the balancing acts of life. They're not always going to be easy, but if you don't watch out, you might lose the hope and vision that got you two together in the first place.

The passion, excitement, fulfillment, and abundant joy that you're supposed to experience in your relationship does not have to be over. Nor does it have to take a back seat to the duties of what it takes to run a family and live a fulfilled life. You can still honor and respect your spouse while dreaming about a brighter future. You can still do things together and walk through life together. But, you must learn how to manage the competing demands of life. That is the critical distinction between strong relationships and weak ones.

Most people prefer to complain rather than target, attack, and subdue the challenges that they are having with the person they have been connected to by God. It's much easier for us to sit back and tell our spouse everything that's wrong with him or her instead of seeking to understand why they are the way they are.

It still amazes me to this day, after all the years that I've been attending church on Sundays, how many people I've seen go to the altar, extend all kinds of grace and mercy to crack addicts, thieves, cheaters, and liars — give miles of compassion to people stuck in destructive cycles, toxic habits, and wild perversions — and then go right back to the pew where their spouse sits and *still* be unwilling to give him or her an inch of grace or mercy.

What happened to grace in the home? What happened to the forgiveness that you gave him or her when you were dating? Why do you now only extend it to everyone else except the very one you're in covenant with?

What if God got tired of forgiving you?

What kind of spiritual relationship would you have if God attacked you for everything that HE didn't like about you, instead of covering and forgiving you? The fact is, our marriages are supposed to *mirror* the relationship between Jesus and the church. Husband, the way Jesus treats the church is how you are supposed to treat your wife. Wife, the way you respect Jesus is how you're supposed to respect your husband. Until your relationship is played out like Christ and the church, all you will have is a broken mirror. And to this day, I don't think anyone has ever had a clear vision of bold dreams through a cracked and crumbling mirror.

Your marital goal should be to mirror Christ. If someone never hears a preacher, or picks up a Bible, or watches a Christian show on TV, they should at least be able to look at your marriage and discover the affection that Jesus and the church have for one other. That's what God designed marriage to be.

Have you lost focus in your marriage? Have the demands of life caused you to lose your desire to pour out God's sacrificial, unconditional love to your spouse-for-life? Is your marriage experiencing a dry spell?

There is good news! Through obedience to God you will discover the remedy for every parched area in your marriage. Come together and drink from the Well, the Word of God, that will never run dry. It is time. Let Jesus restore the life and vibrancy to your marital love.

Acknowledgments

We first and foremost want to thank our Lord and Savior Jesus Christ for his strength and guidance in the writing of this book.

We have been extremely well-served by Etienne Toussaint for keeping the book engaging, focused, and well structured. His gift for writing has blessed us tremendously.

We also want to thank the countless couples that have modeled wholesome Godly marriages, as well as those who have trusted us to advise and coach them on their marital journey. Without your diligent pursuit of a biblical marriage, trust that transcends the natural mind, and undying commitment to your wedding vows, we would have never discovered our own purpose. Both of us are in awe of the invaluable lessons that God has taught us in forgiveness, pain, reconciliation and grace as we have listened to your stories. Our greatest joy has been walking side-by-side with couples and watching their marriages be transformed by God's Word as they have chosen to heal and flourish during some of the most heart-wrenching seasons.

You all are our constant reminder that marriage is indeed a *wholly* hook-up -- two whole people, submitted to the leadership of our Holy God.

About the Authors

Married for 30 years, Dr. T. Cedric and his wife Bobette are the founders of Marriage: The Wholly Hook-up®, a biblically-based teaching forum that *"helps singles get ready and marrieds keep it steady."* They are experts on encouraging and inspiring authentic and transparent dialogue on relationship growth, development, and consistency. Through their dynamic speaking and coaching programs, they have helped countless individuals and married couples find greater fulfillment in their personal relationships, better understanding of their spouse, and thrive inside of their marriage. The Browns are guaranteed to challenge you to step outside of your box so that you can grow for the betterment of both yourself and/or your marriage.

A published author and associate pastor of Greater Mount Calvary Holy Church in Washington, D.C., Dr. T. Cedric Brown is considered one of the nation's leading authorities on Visionary Servant Leadership. As Founder of The Institute for World-Class Leaders, a global training and coaching company, Dr. Brown's expertise is in building world-class organizations that empower world-class servant leaders and teams to advance a world-class vision. He is also a certified John Maxwell speaker, trainer and coach.

Dr. Brown holds a BA in Industrial Engineering from North Carolina A&T State University, an MA in Counseling and Human Services from Regent University, and a DMin in Leadership Development and Organizational Dynamics from United Theological Seminary.

Bobette Brown is the CEO of BGB Enterprises. A former Army 82nd Airborne Paratrooper, she is an international speaker, best-selling author, ICF certified coach, and professional overcomer. She is an Executive Director on The John Maxwell Team and a leadership & personal growth champion who teaches others how to leverage their experiences, live authentically and become the people they were created to be.

She holds a BA in Business Management from the University of Maryland University College, and a MA in Theological Studies from Wesley Theological Seminary. She is a certified Human Behavior Consultant and a Work-Life Certified Professional.